T0196524

SAMSON

THE MODERN-DAY AMERICA
IS AMERICA DOOMED?

STEPHEN R. WILLIAMS

SAMSON THE MODERN-DAY AMERICA
IS AMERICA DOOMED?

iUniverse books may be ordered through booksellers or by contacting:

iUniverse
1663 Liberty Drive
Bloomington, IN 47403
www.iuniverse.com
1-800-Authors (1-800-288-4677)

ISBN: 978-1-5320-5530-0 (sc)
ISBN: 978-1-5320-5563-8 (e)

Library of Congress Control Number: 2018909669

Print information available on the last page.

iUniverse rev. date: 08/29/2018

DEDICATION

To my friend and pastor, the late Reverend Jerry Amstutz, who has gone to be with the Lord Jesus. At the age of ten, I was saved under his preaching, and he was the person who introduced me to Samson when I was a child. I followed him for over forty years and received counseling, spiritual guidance and wisdom, and just some good old friendship from him.

I would also like to extend a big thank you to Reverend Amstutz's wife, Helen, who unselfishly allowed him time to spend with me.

ACKNOWLEDGEMENT

In the fall of 2006, I took a day of vacation. I was listening to the radio, and a man named Charles Swindoll, a great Bible teacher, came on the air. He was teaching about Samson that day.

I listened with great interest while he was teaching. He made this statement about Judges 15:20, "It appears that Samson went straight for 20 years without following his fleshy desires."

When Charles Swindoll made this statement, I felt that a light had come on for me regarding all of the information I had about Samson, and it seemed as though I had found the missing link for how to start writing this book.

I want to give you, Charles Swindoll, the credit for teaching God's Word and letting God work through you to help many others and me.

It is amazing how God works through his Spirit to reach and teach others including people we never see.

Thank you again, Charles Swindoll.

I would also like to give a Big "Thank You" and "Appreciation" to a Great Man of GOD: A Preacher, a Pastor and a former Pastor, who worked several years with Dr. Billy Graham, and a man whom I considered a "Spiritual Daddy" Dr. C. B. Hogue, more commonly called Brother Bill. He just up and volunteered to help edit my book and give me guidance on better ways to word some things and what to leave out or change. He was a great encourager! He has since gone on home to be with the Lord, but his loving, understanding, and encouraging spirit is still with me, Thank you again, Brother Bill.

REVIEWS FOR
SAMSON: THE MODERN-DAY
AMERICA

Stephen Williams has written a book just like the prophets of the Old Testament. He has heard the Word of the Lord our God and has obeyed by writing it out for us, to warn us, to help us. Just like the prophet Ezekiel, who foretold the "wrath of God" on his chosen people, the Jews, Stephen proceeds to shine light in the darkness. There are those who are still listening for the voice of God.

When we ask ourselves, can one person make a difference? The answer is clear. If that one person has confessed "Yes, Lord," he or she has all authority to confess gratefulness and praise to God Almighty for creating a pathway on which the freedoms we hold dear in America can continue. Only a true friendship with Jesus can satisfy this need on a personal and global level. This is possible for you.

Stephen's work is a direct reflection of God's grace in America today. The writing style is simple to comprehend, the appreciation of creation is clear; and the message is repeated throughout the book. Will you choose Jesus, or will you choose yourself? Your blood will not be on Stephen's hands when we all show up at the judgment seat. In what condition will your hands be?

—Teri Lerch
Tulsa, OK

Letter to the author:

Dear Steve,

I read your book with great interest, and although I've had a strong feeling that various large segments of our society are abusing people, our laws, and the constitution, it never occurred to me that our current situation comprises a parallelism with the worst phases of Samson's life.

After thinking back to the earlier years of my life and comparing situations, attitudes, and behaviors with the present, I have identified several things that stand out in stark contrast with the 1930s and 1940s. I think that most of the mischief began in the 1960s, and a few of my pet peeves are listed below. They fit in with your thesis.

- Judges that legislate from the bench and introduce changes to our laws, a process that is not condoned by the US Constitution
- Public schools that misinform (teach a false version of our country's history) and fail utterly to produce graduates suited to assume roles as informed citizens
- So-called university scientists who plagiarize shamelessly and rail bitterly when they get caught.
- So-called environmental scientists who fudge data (lie) to make a study's results conform to their personal leanings or politics. I was taught that it was a cardinal, intellectual sin to influence the scientific process and that if one did, he or she was no longer a scientist but a propagandist.
- The demonizing and hazing of Christians, which has become a cruel sport among left-leaning individuals, especially around Christmas time
- The curse of political correctness police (This asinine practice causes airport security people to call aside an eighty-five-year-old woman and subject her to a body search. That really contributes to air travel safety. PC also results in establishing quotas.)
- The craze for the "redistribution of wealth." Why is it that it's always someone else's wealth they are talking about?

Thanks,

Bill Pogue

Former Astronaut

CONTENTS

INTRODUCTION

I was ten years old when I first read about Samson. I was impressed by what I read, especially that he slew a lion with his bare hands, that he slew one thousand men with the jawbone of a donkey, and that he carried those city gates to a place thirty miles away. Proverbs 20:29 says that the glory of young men is their strength. As a ten-year-old kid, strength was very impressive to me. I kept reading about Samson over and over again. Samson and I, it seemed, became good friends, good buddies. When I got to junior high school, whenever someone would start using foul language, I would picture Samson with the jawbone of a donkey swinging at a thousand men, and I would start swinging, in my mind, at those words and repeat the phrase, *Samson killed them all. Samson killed them all.* I would use that mental image to keep all the bad words out of my mind. I would always keep my Bible marked at the fourteenth, fifteenth, and sixteenth chapters of Judges, which is where Samson's story is told. Sometimes in church, other youngsters would start scuffling and laughing, and to keep myself from laughing, I would open up my Bible and start reading about Samson, taking my mind off of whatever was making the kids laugh. In that way, Samson's story kept me out of a lot of trouble. As time went on, I read more and more about Samson. The more I read about him, the more I liked him. There's just something about him that is of interest to me.

I have noticed that, over the years, many speakers from church pulpits do not have too much good to say about Samson. They frequently refer to him in a negative light, and I always felt that I was the only person who liked Samson. I wrote up a little exercise called "Are You a Samson or a Paul?" in which being a spirit-filled Christian is compared with being a flesh-filled Christian. I concede that Samson operated most of the time in his flesh and not in the Spirit of God. As you turn the pages and start reading about Samson, also consider modern-day America; better yet, see if you can compare modern-day America with the way Samson lived his life.

Here is a little joke about Samson: Did you know that Samson was the biggest comedian in the Bible? He brought down the entire house.

P.S.: Near the end of the book look for the "not very funny" thought of this little wit.

A Paraphrase of Matthew 5:29

If thy "I" causes you to sin,

cast it out and repent. It is better to die to self, than to

have the whole body and soul cast into hell.

"If we abide by the principles taught in the Bible, our country will go on prospering and to prosper; but if we and our posterity neglect its instructions and counsel, there is no telling how great a catastrophe shall come upon us and bury our glory in profound obscurity."

-Daniel Webster

CHAPTER 1

IN THE BEGINNING

Genesis 1:1—"In the beginning ..."
Genesis 1:1—"In the beginning God ..."
Genesis 1:1—"In the beginning God created ..."
Genesis 1:26–27—"In the beginning God created man in His own image ..."
Genesis 2:7—"In the beginning God breathed into man His spirit or the breath of life."
"In the beginning was the word (Jesus Christ) and the word was with God and the word was God.... All things were made by Him" (John 1:1–3 (King James Version, or KJV).).

In short, anyone who claims not to believe in God or who says that there is no God is really saying no to God. James 2:19 says that even the Devil and the demons know and believe in God, but they said no to God.

Psalm 14:1 and 53:1, in the original Hebrew, says, "The fool has said in his heart, no to God."

The word "heart" in Hebrew means "intellect." People who say no to God are saying no based on their intellect. They are not aware of the fact that they are agreeing with Proverbs 16:25.

The *Henry Morris Study Bible* explains it this way: "Atheists and pantheists are mere fools in the sight of the omniscient God regardless of their intellectual achievements. The delusion that this intricately complex cosmos, with its multitudes of marvelously designed living creatures, could have evolved itself by chance is absurd in the highest degree. Psalm 53 is almost an exact replica of this psalm. Also Psalm 14:1–3 is quoted (in effect, not verbatim) in Romans 3:10–12. Evidently the Holy Spirit considers it important to emphasize that those who seek to replace the God of creation with a humanistic or pantheistic philosophy—no matter how wise they profess themselves to be—are really fools in God's sight (note also Romans 1:21–23)."[1]

In 1 Corinthians 6:19–20 (New Living Translation, or NLT), Paul says, "Don't you realize that your body is the temple of the Holy Spirit, who lives in you and was given to you by God? You do not belong to yourself, for God bought you with a high price. So you must honor God with your body." Furthermore, Romans 1:18–20 declares that we are without excuse for not knowing that God exists.

Quoting from the *Henry Morris Study Bible*, "Romans 1:21–28 describes the awful descent of the ancient world from their ancestral knowledge of the true God, as received from Father Noah, down into evolutionary pantheism and its accompanying polytheism (1:21–25) and then into the gross immorality and wickedness that inevitably follows such apostasy. Those who deny the God of creation are fools (Ps. 14:1) and 'without a defense'.... Yet they come to such a foolish decision in the foolish belief that they are scientific in trying to explain the infinitely complex, majestic, beautiful creation without a Creator. The ancient pagans did this, with immeasurably tragic results in the history of the human race. Modern evangelicals are in serious danger of starting down that same slippery slope, compromising with evolutionism and increasingly flirting with New Age pantheism, feminism, and occultism. Compare 2 Timothy 3:1–13."[2]

All the Scriptures above show us that God created all things, including humanity. God put His Spirit in each person, and humanity is under His power and subject to His regulations.

---

[1] From the *Henry Morris Study Bible* by Henry Morris, First Printing 2012; pages 836–37. Used with permission from the publisher, Master Books®, a division of the New Leaf Publishing Group, Inc.

[2] Morris, 1701.

Genesis 1:2 says that "darkness was upon the face of the earth," and in verse 3, God creates light. When you read verses 5–31, you see that after every day of creation, the Bible says the evening, or night, and the morning, or day, was a day. Notice in verse 2 that darkness was first on the face of the earth, and then light entered. Darkness came first and then the light after every day of creation. This all ties in with the fact that we are all born in darkness or sin, and when we come to accept Jesus as the Lord of our life, light—a new day—dawns.

When the prophet Daniel was in the lions' den, it was dark at first, but his trust and faith in God turned the situation into one of light. When Jesus was on the cross, it was the darkest day in His life, but His obedience to God's will turned it into the brightest (or "lightest") day for all humanity.

In the Old Testament, Samson's life turned to darkness when he disobeyed God. After his confession and repentance, he saw the light.

Our world is getting darker and darker because we are going by man's rules and not God's. But if we will turn back to God, we will get lighter (John 3:18–21).

Going back a step or two from Genesis 1:1–2, we can get a picture of what God first had in His plans. Some theologians teach that there was a heaven and that there were angels in heaven before the creation of the world and man. The highest and most beautiful angel was one named Lucifer. Everything was on the "light" side (Is. 14:12–17), but Lucifer wanted to be like God. His pride was sinful, and he was thrown out of heaven. The darkness on the earth in Genesis 1:2 came about because of Lucifer's sin.

Notice these interesting things about Lucifer: The name *LucIfer* has an *I* right in the center of it. He developed an attribute called prIde, which also has an *I* in the center of it. This pride led to a disease called sIn, and he became the father of a sin called a *LIE*, both of which have an*I* right at their centers. In other words, Lucifer (Satan) had an *I* problem. His *I*, or *self*, was in charge of his life rather than God.

If you start with his name and write the other words below it, it will look like this.

Notice, if you please, that Lucifer started out big, but with his *I* problem, he wound up small.

LucIfer   first

prIde   second

sIn	third
lIe	fourth
I	fifth

This pattern was also Samson's problem, and it is the problem that America has today. I believe we are down to the fourth level or step on the depiction above. We are one step away from receiving God's judgment and wrath if we do not repent.

Remember that before sin came into the world, everything was light, bright, glorious, and good. Sin brought the darkness.

When Jesus (the Light of the World) comes back to this world of darkness to rule again, it will be all glory and light again, forever and ever. Amen. John 8:12 (Amplified Bible, or AB) says, "Once more Jesus addressed the crowd. He said, I am the Light of the world. He who follows Me will not be walking in the dark, but will have the Light which is Life."

Jesus Christ is the light that giveth light to every man (see John 1:9a). "There it was—the true Light [was then] coming into the world [the genuine, perfect, steadfast Light] that illumines every person" (John 1:9b AB). Compare this with Isaiah 49:6. "He says, It is too light a thing that you should be My servant to raise up the tribes of Jacob and to restore the survivors [of the judgments] of Israel; I will also give you for a light to the nations, that My salvation may extend to the end of the earth" (AB).

So wake up, America! Jesus is our light in all this darkness. Let's confess our darkness, repent of our sins, and believe in, trust in, rely on, and glorify the Man in the Glory—

JESUS CHRIST!

CHAPTER 2

INTRODUCTION TO THE LIFE OF SAMSON

Romans 15:4 (AB) says, "For whatever was thus written in former days was written for our instruction, that by [our steadfast and patient] endurance and the encouragement [drawn] from the Scriptures we might hold fast to and cherish hope." Also, 1 Corinthians 10:11 (AB) says, "Now these things befell them by way of a figure [as an example and warning to us]; they were written to admonish and fit us for right action by good instruction, we in whose days the ages have reached their climax (their consummation and concluding period)." Keep these thoughts in mind as you read this chapter and see what instructions, encouragement, warnings, and lessons God shows you.

Samson was ordained by God when he was born to be a Nazirite and to judge and rule the Philistines. Samson's parents were praying to God to have a child and had told God that if He would give them one, they would dedicate the child to the service of the Lord. When Samson was born, he was given the Nazirite vow. There were three main parts of the vow that Samson had to follow. One of them was that he had to abstain from any kind of wine—even grape juice or grape vines. The second was that he was not to touch or eat anything that was unclean, and the third part of his vow was that he would refrain from cutting the seven locks of his hair. His hair had to remain long.

When America began as a nation, the people came to this land because they wanted a place to worship and serve God freely. Just as Samson was born to serve God, America was born as a place to serve God. When the settlers came over to build America, there were rules and requirements to follow, which were God's rules and laws—the Bible. Prayer was openly practiced, and God's commandments were observed and became a part of ordinary life. Samson was God's man, and America is for Christian believers, who are God's people.

The Nazirite vow was said for a person to be totally dedicated to God. See Numbers 6:1–8 for the vow requirements. The phrase "the Spirit of the Lord came upon Samson" appears in the Bible several times, and the internal phrase "Spirit of the Lord" indicates the progression of the anointing of the Lord. So we see that several times through Samson's life, he had the anointing of God on him.

Interestingly, 1 Corinthians 11:14 says that even nature itself or common sense indicates that if a man has long hair, it is a shame and disgrace to him. If long hair was a shame and a disgrace, why did Samson have it? The main reason was to keep him in a humble spirit; in those days, it was shameful for him to go out in public with long hair. In other words, part of the Nazirite vow was intended to keep Samson humble before God.

As we can see here, Samson was born and dedicated to God. In Judges 13:25, we see the spirit of the Lord beginning to move in Samson and making ready to start his life mission: to judge and rule over the Philistines.

CHAPTER 3

THE LIFE OF SAMSON

And [Samson] judged (defended) Israel in the days of the
Philistines twenty years.

—Judges 15:20 AB

How many times in life have you been given a task or a job to do with
instructions how to do it?

We think we know how to do it, and we think our way is better than
the Bosses' way or the instructions.

Example: We buy something that we have to assemble. We don't use the
instructions on how to assemble it. It doesn't work quite right, so we have to
get the instructions out and start all over again.

Or the Boss gives us a job to do and tells us what to do or not to do. We
think we know all about it, and ignoring his rules we do it our way. When
the job is completed it is not quite right. So we wind up in the Bosses office
with a little talking to and maybe a reprimand.

This is how Samson starts out his life. He does what he wants to do and
how he wants to do it. He does not pay attention to the ways and instructions
that God gives him.

As you read this chapter, notice how Samson starts out on the wrong foot and does not change feet or get in step with God. This is how he goes about his entire life.

Notice Samson liked doing things his way to please his self, but did not like it when the Philistines did things to please themselves. Samson did not know it but he was proving Romans 2:1 to be right.

The last verse of Judges 13 tells us that the "Spirit of the Lord" began to move and stir in Samson. However, the first thing Samson did was go down to the Philistines, his enemies, to find a woman there and fell in love with her. (Or should I say that he fell "in lust" with her?) When Samson told his parents that he wanted her, his parents urged him not to take her as a wife because she was from the enemy camp. But Samson wouldn't listen to his parents. He said, "Get her for me because she pleaseth me well."

As we can already see, Samson started out on the wrong path by seeking his own will instead of God's will for his life. As we continue with Samson's story, we will find out that he never did get married.

One day, Samson was walking with his parents through the vineyard, and a lion roared and attacked Samson. In response, Samson killed the lion with his bare hands. The Bible says that the Spirit of the Lord came upon him mightily, meaning that the anointing of the Lord came upon Samson.

Over in 1 Peter 5:8, the author declares that the Devil goes around like a roaring lion, seeking whom he may devour. Satan was already trying to kill God's man. Since Samson was not supposed to touch anything unclean, which a dead lion would be, this lion could have been Satan attacking Samson, trying to weaken him further after he compromised himself by being in the flesh and lusting after this woman.

Some days later, as Samson walked by the body of the lion he had killed, he saw honey in its mouth. Samson very carefully put his hand in the lion's mouth, making sure not to touch the lion's body. He touched only the honey, but the honey was touching the dead lion, which is unclean. Again, Samson is playing with fire; he is compromising. In Proverbs 6:27–28, we read, "Can a man take fire into his bosom and not get burned? Can a man walk on hot coals and his feet not get burned?" Solomon meant, "Can a man play with sin and not be affected?" The answer is no.

Samson's playing with sin is the beginning of his weakening, but he keeps on going. He went to see his wife-to-be, made a feast, and put forth a riddle to the thirty men who were there. If they could guess his riddle, he would give each of them a suit of clothes. However, they could not guess his riddle. One of the men went to Samson's wife-to-be and asked her to learn the answer. If not, he said, "We will burn you and your father's house with fire." So she went to Samson and wept, which led Samson to finally give in and tell her the secret. She, naturally, told the man, and the men approach Samson with the solution to the riddle. Of course, Samson got very angry. He went to a town called Ashkelon and slew thirty men to pay for his garments. Ashkelon was one of five cities that comprised Philistine and its citizens were believers of the false god Dagon. One interesting aspect of this story (Judg. 14:19) is that the thirty men of Ashkelon had nothing to do with the wedding, yet God gave Samson the power to slay thirty of them to pay his debt.

Samson cooled off and went back home to his parents. He returned later to get his wife around the time the wheat would be harvested. When he got there, he found out that the father of his fiancée had given her to another man because he didn't think that Samson cared about her. This angered Samson, so he went out and caught three hundred foxes, tied them tail to tail in pairs, put a fiery torch in the tails of each pair, and set them loose in the grain fields of the Philistines, which, in turn, burned the fields. Samson thought he was blameless. He was simply thinking of the Old Testament law, "An eye for an eye, and a tooth for a tooth." This is an expression of his attitude. When the Philistines learned what Samson had done and why he had done it, they kept their word and burned Samson's fiancée and her father in their house. Samson never married her, but he went on to judge, defend, and rule Israel in the days of the Philistines for twenty years.

The next recorded event in Samson's life involved three thousand men from Judah who were of his own people. They announced that they intended to turn Samson over to the Philistines, and he, naively, asked them to swear that they would not harm him. They promised, and Samson believed them. Then they bound Samson up with some rope and took him to the Philistines, who saw the group approaching. Again, the Spirit of the Lord came mightily upon Samson; he broke the ropes off of his arms, found a fresh donkey jawbone, and with it, he slew a thousand men.

Considering that Samson was not supposed to touch anything dead or unclean, did he do anything wrong by picking up the jawbone of a donkey to slay a thousand men? In the tenth and eleventh chapters of the Book of Acts, God told Peter three times to rise and eat some food, and each time Peter replied that it was unclean. God said, "What I call clean, don't call unclean." So in Samson's case, when the Spirit of the Lord came upon him to slay these men, it appears that, this time, God had made it acceptable.

Again, maybe Satan was trying to trip Samson up with this unclean jawbone. Satan is always trying to confuse us and mix us up in our spiritual lives. However, this could be one of those times when Satan meant something for bad but God meant it for good. As Christians and Americans, we need more discernment in our lives.

Notice that when Samson was getting the honey from the dead, unclean lion, he knew in his spirit that he was not supposed to be doing that but wanted to see how close to the fire or sin he could get without getting burned. With the donkey jawbone, he was trying to save his own life, and when he had successfully defended himself, he threw it away and never had anything else to do with it.

"And [Samson] judged (defended) Israel in the days of the Philistines twenty years" (Judg. 15:20 AB).

This little fact about some of Samson's feats is interesting. In the beginning of his story, he took the three parts of the Nazirite vow; later there were thirty men at the festival feast; after that, he used three hundred foxes to get revenge; and then he was approached by three thousand men of Judah. The recurring three in those numbers could be symbolic of the three points of his vow.

Now, a little review of Samson's story so far—his big weakness was not women, necessarily, but self; he had an *I* problem. He wanted to do things his way and not God's way. The first girl that Samson saw was from the enemy's camp, but Samson wanted her. When he burned the fields ready for harvest with the three hundred foxes, he justified it with the Old Testament law regarding an eye for an eye and a tooth for a tooth. Samson always played with sin and was constantly tempted. Remember the warning in Proverbs: "Can a man take fire in his bosom and his clothes not be burned?" Samson was bound to get burned.

Many pulpit speakers think that Samson's big sin or weakness was women, whereas I believe that Samson's weakness with women was really the fruit of his personal sin—*self.* Samson always thought about himself. Samson wanted what Samson wanted. After he had slain a thousand men, he was thirsty and started crying to God, "Am I going to die of thirst now?" All Samson thought about was himself. This prayer marks the first recorded time that he prayed to God.

CHAPTER 4

THE DOWNFALL OF SAMSON

We have probably heard the example about putting a frog in a pot of water and turning the fire on low. AS the water slowly gets hot, the frog's body slowly adjusts to the heat. He does not jump out of the water because he keeps adjusting to the heat; he finally gets burned to death.

This example is what about to happen to Samson. He keeps playing with sin, he keeps adjusting his conscience to the sinful situations and instead of getting away from them he finally gets captured.

In the last verse of the fifteenth chapter of Judges, we read, "Samson judged Israel for twenty years in the days of the Philistines." This could be interpreted to mean that Samson finally "went good" and maintained it for twenty years. For all of those years, nothing bad was said or, at least, written about him. But then, chapter 16 informs us that Samson went to Gaza, saw a harlot, went in, and spent the night with her.

In chapter 16 Verse 2-3 we read that after Samson visited the Harlot, he arose at midnight, pulled up the gates door, post and all, and carried them to the top of a hill in Hebron, some 38-40 miles all uphill. What strength God bestowed on Samson!

The size of the gates from some records were approximately ten feet by ten feet and anywhere from 18 to 36 inches thick, covered with bronze or iron, remember the Philistines has the monopoly on iron, and weighed as much as 5000 pounds or more.

Think how much energy it took to pull up the gates and all the parts, put them on his shoulders carry them uphill 38-40 miles uphill, nonstop. It took approximately 18-20 hours, just before sunset that day.

This shows how much strength God gave Samson. This also shows there is no doubt that Samson's God was greater than any of the gods the Philistines had or any other people and their gods.

Yet with all this giftedness of super strength God gave Samson, he still would not repent of his sins of "self-control" and turn to God with all his heart.

Now notice how quick Samson loses this awesome strength to his enemies.

In Hosea 4:11, the prophet Hosea declares that harlotry and wine and new wine will take away a man's heart, or a man's spiritual understanding. Samson played with fire by walking through the grape yard. He didn't avoid temptation. It was the custom to have a wedding feast or banquet when a couple was getting married, and it was held at the bride's home, a feast intended to be a happy and joyous occasion. Usually, only men were invited, and even then only a select few. Wine was an important part of the feast. The Bible doesn't say whether Samson did or did not drink any, but it is clear that he did not avoid the appearance of evil.

Samson was guilty of immorality, which Hosea says takes away a person's spiritual understanding. So Samson kept getting weaker and weaker through all of his constant playing with sins.

Finally, Samson meets Delilah—dainty, little, deceitful Delilah, one of the enemies and the main one used to get to him. Samson spent the night with her three times, and the Philistines told her, "If you can discover the source of Samson's strength, we will each give you 1,100 pieces of silver." That delighted Delilah, and she committed to asking Samson from where his strength came.

Three times, Samson lied to Delilah and teased her about his strength. Over in Proverbs 26, verses 18 and 19, it says, "Like a madman who casts firebrands and arrows and death, so is the man who deceives his neighbor and then says, 'Was I not joking?'" The word for *madman* in Hebrew means "insane."

Samson was teasing her in a negative manner because, again, he had this inner pride in his life. The word *pride* has the letter *I* right in the middle of it, and Samson had himself right in the center of his life. Samson's big problem was that he had an *I* problem.

Delilah kept trying. She would get upset and weep before Samson because he would not tell her where his strength came from and would not be honest with her. Even though Delilah was of the enemy and did not accept Samson's God, she still had feelings and got emotionally upset. That means that there was still something alive in her and something missing—a commitment to and a personal relationship with God. Being with the enemy, she could not recognize that.

Delilah continued to pressure Samson day and night until he finally gave in. He told her that his strength was in his hair that had never been cut. With that in mind, Delilah had Samson lay his head on her lap and go to sleep. While he was sleeping, she called a man in to shave the hair off his head. The men brought her the money.

Then the Bible reports that Samson woke up and went outside, not knowing that the Lord had left him. In the past, when Samson would do something important and right before God, the Spirit of the Lord and an anointing would come upon him. This time, the Spirit of God had left him, and Samson didn't recognize it. For such a betrayal, Delilah can be considered the Old Testament's Judas Iscariot because she betrayed God's man, Samson, and turned him over to the enemy just as Judas Iscariot betrayed Jesus and helped turn him over to the enemy. Also, both betrayals were done for money.

When the Philistines captured Samson, they gouged his eyes out and put him to work in prison at a grinding mill. They rejoiced to their god, Dagon, because they believed that he had given the enemy into their hands. Samson was using the remainder of his strength to serve the enemy and not to serve God.

When Samson sinned and the Spirit of God left him, the enemy captured him. Samson had what I call spiritual AIDS. AIDS is a condition in which the immune system of the body ceases to fight off germs and disease, which overtake the body. Our protection is the Holy Spirit of God. If we lose Him, the Enemy comes and captures us. Samson lost God, God left him, and he was captured by the Enemy. Samson had spiritual AIDS. Does America have spiritual AIDS?

Now, what can we Christians in America learn from Samson? When America was settled, the people were with God. Slowly, the country has compromised. We have accepted sin, things that are wrong, and things that were no good from the start. We compromised a little at a time just as Samson did. We even play with the Enemy as Samson did. We go through everyday life trying to please ourselves and not God.

A key verse in the Book of Judges that seems to fit America is 17:6, which says, "In these days there is no king in Israel and every man did what was right in his own eyes." Samson always did what was right in his eyes. Samson wanted to please Samson. Likewise, people in America today want to do what is right in their own eyes and please themselves.

Remember that the Enemy does not have the word *compromise* in its vocabulary. Notice how persistently Delilah kept asking to find out where Samson's weakness was. She was committed and determined, and she finally brought him down.

This is the kind of commitment and dedication we Christians need for God. Also, remember that this warfare we are in is not of the flesh and blood but against spiritual wickedness. (See Ephesians 6:12.) This is all the more reason that we need to repent and get back with God.

America has one of the strongest if not the strongest military groups in the world. Just like Samson, the strongest military man for God in His time America will lose all of her power and be captured by the enemy if we do not repent and come back to trusting in God instead of man. We will be destroyed from within, instead of outside force, like what happened to Samson.

CHAPTER 5

THE TREE OF LIFE

You may recall that the fruit in the Garden of Eden that caused all the problems was the "pair" on the ground. Remember, any fruit that is on the ground is not on the tree, will not grow to full maturity, and will stay on the ground and finally rot.

In the center of the Garden of Eden was the Tree of Life (Gen. 2:9). The Tree of Life symbolized access to eternal life, for which Jesus Christ is our hope. In John 15, Jesus says that He is the vine and that, if we want to grow and mature and produce fruit, we have to abide in Him and unite with Him.

Jesus Christ is our tree of life. Samson did not stay near the tree of life. Instead, he walked off and did things his way. He did not keep his commitment of serving God.

America is away from the tree of life, Jesus Christ. We are doing things our way and not for Jesus, the same thing Samson did. We are walking away from the tree of life and Jesus and doing things our own way. We are not growing or maturing spiritually, and we are making a rotten mess of our lives and of our nation just as Samson made a rotten mess of his life for God and his nation.

Today, many Christians and many contemporary people have mind-sets of their own. They keep tinkering with and reading the Bible in an attempt to get the Bible to justify their own tastes and their own wishes, sort of like Samson did. The underlying ideas are that we are intelligent and that we know what should be said and how it should be said. Instead of listening to what the Bible says and letting the Bible be our authority as the Word of God, we try to trim it down to fit our own personal ideals and our own personal ways. Such thinking and tampering with the text is the occupation of unwise people.

CHAPTER 6

WHAT OTHER MEN IN THE BIBLE HAD TO SAY

In the book of the prophet Amos, God points out that the people of certain places have sinned again and again and says that He will not forget it. America is like that. We have sinned again and again, and God will not forget it. Amos 3:3 asks, "How can two walk together unless they agree?" Jesus said that a nation divided cannot stand. Samson was divided between himself and God, and America, we are divided between selfish things and God or between man's ways and God's ways.

Amos 3:6 says, "When a disaster comes to a city, is it not because the Lord planned it?" Are some of the destructive events that America has faced and is facing occurring because God planned them in response to our sins, to our saying no to God's way and yes to man's way?

Samson kept encountering obstacles in his life because he kept on sinning. He would not stay with God. With all the problems we have in America today, we still do not return to God for help. We still attempt to find some way—through science or humanity—to justify all of our wrongdoings. Again in Amos, in verses 1 and 2 of the eighth chapter, the prophet talks about ripe fruit, speaking of the fruit of the tree, and declares that it is ripe for punishment. The fruit is symbolic of Israel. This fruit we have from "our" tree of life is ripe for punishment and for God's judgment on America unless we repent and get back with God.

In 1 Chronicles 10:13–14, we learn that Saul died because he would not keep God's Word, even seeking mediums instead of inquiring of God. In America, how much do we seek the opinions of people? America is slowly dying because we are not seeking God.

In Hosea 4:6, God says his people are destroyed for a lack of knowledge of Him. The more we keep God out of our lives, the more sure we will be judged and destroyed by God, guaranteed.

Nehemiah 1:8 explains that if we sin, God will scatter us. Today, America is sinning, and we are being scattered. Nehemiah also said that if we would turn to God, He would bring us back to His chosen place. Proverbs 3:5 tells us "to trust in the Lord with all your heart and lean not on your own understanding." We are prone to relying on our human understanding and not God's. That is human wisdom; godly wisdom is in relying on what God says. Proverbs 16:25 says, "There's a way that seemeth right unto man but the end thereof are the ways of death." America loves to do that which seems right to man.

This ties in with 2 Timothy 4:3–4 about men who do not want to hear the truth, instead wanting to hear things that tickle their ears. They want to rely on human wisdom and not godly wisdom because godly wisdom requires a sacrifice (dying to self and making a commitment of the heart to God). Just as Samson didn't want to make such a sacrifice, we just do not want to do it. Also notice what the prophet Jeremiah says in Jeremiah 5:30–31 (AB), "An appalling and horrible thing [bringing desolation and destruction] has come to pass in the land: The prophets prophesy falsely, and the priests exercise rule at their own hands *and* by means of the prophets. And My people love to have it so! But what will you do when the end comes?"

Does America really want to be captured by the Enemy the way Samson was and let the Enemy run us? America will if we don't return to God.

In Micah 4:5, the New Living Translation, reads, "Even though nations around us worship idols, we will follow the Lord our God forever and ever." Is America willing to do that? In John 8:15 (AB), it reads, "You [set yourselves up to] judge according to the flesh (by what you see). [You condemn by external, human standards.]" We impose too much by human standards and not by what God says.

Zachariah 7:6 (NLT) reads, "And even now in your holy festivals, you don't think about me but only of pleasing yourself." Today's churches have too many activities designed to please people or to bring people into the church life. We spend too much time talking about all the good things and services we do and very little time in true worship to God. Church leaders often say nothing about meeting with the church to please or worship God. We are doing things to tickle men's ears, as Timothy says. In the end times, people don't want to hear the truth.

It looks like America does not want to hear the truth, but if we keep going like this, we will soon be like Samson—grinding the mill, the food for our enemy, and losing all of our freedoms and rights. The only thing left will be what's in our hearts. If we're imprisoned by the enemies, we can't produce too much for God. The Holy Spirit needs to be our guide, but we do not believe in, rely on, or trust in Him or in God; we rely on ourselves. This, according to 2 Timothy 4:3–4, is the definition of being "politically correct." Note what Isaiah 30:8–11 (AB) states.

> Now, go, write it before them on a tablet and inscribe it in a book, that it may be as a witness for the time to come forevermore. For this is a rebellious people, faithless *and* lying sons, children who will not hear the law *and* instruction of the Lord; Who [virtually] say to the seers [by their conduct], See not! and to the prophets, Prophesy not to us what is right! Speak to us smooth things, prophesy deceitful illusions. Get out of the true way, turn aside out of the path, cease holding up before us the Holy One of Israel.

John 16:9 states that the sin of the world, including America, is unbelief—not relying on or trusting in God. In short, we say no to God and yes to self.

We need to learn what real worship is and get back to offering that to God. Real worship to God involves reviving and making our conscience alive by the holiness of God with a reverent devotion and humble spirit toward God. We need to nourish our minds with God's truth, cleanse our thoughts with the splendor and grace of God, open our hearts to God's love, and die to our own will, learning and accepting the will and purpose of God.

Worship is the giving up of *all* of ourselves and our nature to God. In short, worship is saying no to self and yes to God. If we go to a worship service, have a good time, and enjoy everything and everybody but have no real change in our life, we really had no worship. We need to make an urgent appeal to everyone to get back to truly worshipping God. How? With a renewed life in the power of Jesus Christ. We need to meditate on Christ, His beauty, His purpose and will, and His love for our lives.

"And [Samson] judged (defended) Israel in the days of the Philistines twenty years" (Judg. 15:20 AB).

CHAPTER 7

WHERE DID SAMSON GO WRONG?

One way Samson went wrong was he started out by leaving his heritage of a Godly home to a life of making himself in charge of his life and leaving God out of his life. He also disobeyed his parents by choosing a girl outside his covenant people. He did not ask them if he could marry her, he told them.

How did Samson go wrong after twenty years of apparently good living during which nothing bad was recorded about him. Although America had been living well for roughly two hundred years, from the time that America was founded until after the end of the Civil War, we have moved toward the wrong. How have we gone wrong? How did Samson go wrong? How was Samson overcome by the prostitute in Gaza and by Delilah?

The answer can be found in Luke's Gospel. In Luke 11:23 (AB), Jesus says, "He who is not with Me [siding and believing with Me] is against Me, and he who does not gather with Me [engage in My interest], scatters." Then in verses 24–26, Jesus continued.

> When the unclean spirit has gone out of a person, it roams
> through waterless places in search [of a place] of rest (release,
> refreshment, ease); and finding none it says, I will go back
> to my house from which I came. And when it arrives, it

finds [the place] swept and put in order and furnished and decorated. And it goes and brings other spirits, seven [of them], more evil than itself, and they enter in, settle down, and dwell there; and the last state of that person is worse than the first.

Keep in mind that when we sin and do not confess and repent, the sin lies in our spirits and starts a decaying process. In time, it will weaken us spiritually, and finally it will destroy us.

The process is a lot like that of termites destroying a house. If you don't get rid of them and replace the damaged parts, the house will look great on the outside but will get weaker on the inside until the house finally falls down, like what happened to Samson with his unconfessed sins.

When King David committed adultery with Bathsheba, he did not confess his sin at first. This unconfessed sin caused him guilt and led him to sin again in having her husband, Uriah, killed. Then David was guilty of two sins (2 Sam. 11:1–4 and 11:15). The Lord sent the prophet Nathan to David to show him his sins. David finally confessed and repented of his sins (2 Sam. 11, 12).

When we sin, we have to confess the sin, repent of it, and then replace these weaknesses in our spirits with new material, the Word of God, in order to build them up again.

Samson did not, and he fell.

What is America going to do? Are we going to leave our sins alone and then fall or be destroyed from within, or are we going to repent and replace the *I* ways with God's ways?

When Samson sinned, he ignored it. He might have scattered those unclean spirits in him for a short time, but he did not confess his sins, and he did not repent. Samson kept on going. Every time he would do wrong, he would just fluff it off and then try to do good.

In America, we don't admit our sins, our shortcomings, or our wrongdoings. We think that if we sin once but then go out and do two good things, that will eliminate the sin. But it doesn't.

In Galatians 6:7–8, the Bible teaches that when we sow sin, we reap the wrath of God. When we sow good deeds, we get the blessings of God. Blessings do not cancel out the bad. The only thing that will cancel out sin is confessing and repenting of it by the blood of Jesus Christ.

For twenty years, Samson did well. For two hundred years America did well and like Samson, America has not confessed her sins and turned back to God. We just let them sit idle like the unclean spirit, but that unclean spirit comes back. It got into Samson, and it is getting into America because we do not confess our sins, we do not repent, and we do not replace this evil in our lives—the unconfessed and unrepented sins—with God's Word. The evil spirits now are controlling us, and they will continue until we do repent. Christ said, "I tell you, Nay: but, except ye repent, ye shall all likewise perish" (Luke 13:3 KJV).

America, right now, is on the verge of perishing because we do not—will not—repent. We will not give up self and go back to God. Is America going to be like Samson, captured by the enemy, or like the apostle Paul, who works to catch the enemies? Even though they bound him, Paul was still in control. While Samson's life started out in the ways of the flesh, Paul started out in the way of the spirit. Paul denied self. What are we going to do, America?

The garden of Eden is where Adam and Eve sinned, and God had to make a sacrifice for them. They had tried it their way, but it wasn't pleasing to God. Samson tried it his way, but it was not pleasing to God. America has tried it her way, and it is not pleasing to God. We need to be willing to make the sacrifice to cover for our sins.

Paul was willing to make the sacrifice, and Paul made it not for his sins or wrongdoings but for things he was doing right, for following God. One meaning of the term *sacrifice* is "a gift" or "something given to God to express our devotion to Him." The sacrifice Paul made involved giving up his own desires in order to do what God desired. Samson did not do it. This is the sacrifice the people in America need to give God. God wants our devotion—our commitment to Him.

Samson had some forbidden fruit in his life. Is there any forbidden fruit in our lives that we keep tampering with and avoid getting rid of?

> In 2 Peter 1:5–9, the Amplified Bible reads,
> For this very reason, adding your diligence [to the divine promises], employ every effort in exercising your faith to develop virtue (excellence, resolution, Christian energy), and in [exercising] virtue [develop] knowledge (intelligence), and in [exercising] knowledge [develop] self-control, and in [exercising] self-control [develop] steadfastness (patience, endurance), and in [exercising] steadfastness [develop] godliness (piety), and in [exercising] godliness [develop]

brotherly affection, and in [exercising] brotherly affection [develop] Christian love. For as these qualities are yours and increasingly abound in you, they will keep [you] from being idle or unfruitful unto the [full personal] knowledge of our Lord Jesus Christ (the Messiah, the Anointed One). For whoever lacks these qualities is blind, [spiritually] shortsighted, seeing only what is near to him, and has become oblivious [to the fact] that he was cleansed from his old sins.

Here Peter discusses how to grow spiritually: add faith to virtue, knowledge, self-control, steadfastness, brotherly love, and kindness. Add these to your life. And he says that if you add these to your life, they'll keep you fruitful. You will be on the fruit tree of life, Jesus Christ. But if you do not have these qualities, you are going to be shortsighted and blinded; you're going to have doubts and fears about whether you are really saved. Are we really one nation under God? We need to get back to Jesus, to get back to God, and to get out of these confusions and these blind spots in our everyday living.

If you do what verses 5–7 say you should do, you will become like verse 8, or the apostle Paul. If you do not do what verses 5–7 say to do, you will become like verse 9, or Samson. So are you going to be a Samson or a Paul? Are you and is America going to live life in the way of the flesh or the way of the spirit? Some of you church leaders might ask your churches, Is this church a Samson or a Paul? Does the church make decisions based on the Word of God or based on the way that seems right to man?

Is America going to be a Samson or a Paul? Are we going to be a Samson and live by the flesh, or are we going to turn to Christ?

Remember, the word *Christian* has the word *Christ* in it. If you take *Christ* out of the word *Christian*, you have –*ian* left, which stands for "I am nothing." Without Christ, I am nothing. Without Christ as the center of our nation, we are nothing. We will be defeated.

Note the parallels between the life of Samson and the life of Jesus Christ. Both births were foretold by an angel, both were separated from God in the womb, both were Nazirites, both moved in the power of the Holy Spirit, both were rejected by their people, and both destroyed—or will destroy—their enemies. Now look at the contrast between Samson and Jesus. Samson lived a life of sin, but Jesus' life was sinless. Samson, at the time of his death, prayed, "O God, that I may be at once avenged of the Philistines for my two eyes," while Jesus prayed, "Father, forgive them, for they know not what they do." In death, Samson's arms were outstretched in wrath. In death, Jesus's arms were outstretched in love.[3]

Samson died, but Jesus Christ is still alive, still living, still going strong. How much of Samson does America have? Too much. How much of Jesus Christ does America have? Too little.

Does Samson have an end-time message for us? Samson was God's man, and Christians are God's people. Samson sinned for a while and moved away from God, and America has does the same. Samson is captured by the enemy for a time. Will America be captured by the Enemy? God gave Samson victory and took him home. Will Jesus Christ take the Christians in America home and give us victory?

---

[3] J. Vernon McGee, *Thru the Bible Commentary*, volume II, pages 81–82. Used with permission.

CHAPTER 8

WHAT DOES THE PROPHET ISAIAH HAVE TO SAY ABOUT SAMSON AND AMERICA?

Isaiah is normally considered to be the greatest of the Old Testament prophets and is known as the "evangelical prophet." *Isaiah* means "salvation of the Lord." He was the son of Amoz, and he prophesied during the reigns of four kings: Uzziah, Jotham, Ahaz, and Hezekiah. In short, the prophets (from Isaiah to Malachi) were men of God who warned the Israelites of their sins and tried to get them to repent and turn back to God.

When Isaiah stepped into his ministry, Israel—like the United States today—was at a critical place in its history. It was suffering from the fleshy fruits of religious and moral compromise, just as America is today. Isaiah was speaking to Israel, a nation awaiting God's judgment, and America is now awaiting God's judgment.

In chapter 1 of Isaiah, verses 1–2, Isaiah says, "The Lord has spoken to the people, but they have rebelled and broken away from God."

God has spoken to America through churches, preachers, television, radio, books, papers, and magazines. But as a nation, we have rebelled against God and turned or broken away from Him. We as a nation have said no to God. As a nation, we have nourished and raised up a generation of rebellious children.

In verse 3, it looks as though animals are smarter, have more common sense, and know their owners better than man does. From a moral viewpoint, humanity is sliding downward and getting closer to equality with animals. In 1 Corinthians 2:14–16, God tells us that we don't understand Him because we listen to our spirits and not God's Spirit, the way Samson did.

Isaiah 1:4 records Isaiah's telling the Israelites that they are a sinful nation and have gone backward, just as Samson did and America has. In verse 5, Israel is shown to have grieved God, much the same way that both Samson and America have. We have quenched His Spirit (1 Thess. 5:19), and we do not heed His correction. We are a sick and sinful nation.

Since we do not follow God's Spirit, we cannot discern or understand God's ways or plans, and our hearts are hardened (Mark 8:10–18, Acts 7:51). God gives us hope in Hebrews 4:7 and Psalm 95:7–8. Repent, America. Listen to God. He will hear when we are willing to listen.

Isaiah 1:6 declares that we, as a nation, are full of sores, sickness, and wounds inside and out—physically, economically, and spiritually. Samson became that way after committing his big sin. Repent, America, before it is too late.

Verse 7 asks, Is our nation being slowly destroyed, cities being burned, and land being destroyed because we have forgotten God? Repent, America; repent (Luke 13:3, 5). Repent or perish.

Verses 8 and 9 of Isaiah 1 demonstrate how Americans have deserted God and godly living and are against spiritual leaders or others who tell us about God. We would probably have been destroyed long ago if it were not for the few faithful, dedicated, and committed men and women of God. Remember, Samson deserted God, did things his way, and got captured by the enemy. Repent, America.

Verses 10–15 tell of God being sick and tired of our "see what I did" and "what a good boy I am" attitudes. We have too many man-made goodies, and our good is no good (Is. 64:6). We are all talk and no heart for God (1 John 3:18). We have too many unconfessed sins, and one of the most unconfessed sins we have is not forgiving people of their sins. We have turned the Sabbath into a time or day of entertainment instead of worship to God. Remember what real worship is?

In verses 16 and 17, God declares that sin is a reproach to any people (Prov. 14:34b); if we cover or hide our sins, we will not prosper (Prov. 28:13a). God's hand is heavy on us when we keep silent about our sins (Ps. 32: 3, 4) because He wants us to confess them (1 John 1:9), and does not like to destroy His people. He wants us to repent and live (Ez. 33:11).

In verses 18–20, God calls for us to repent of our sins, to become white as snow. If we obey, we will be blessed; if we do not obey, we will receive a curse or God's judgment (Deut. 11:26–28). If we as a nation are going to live or die, the choice or decision is ours. Do we want to go the easy way or the hard way (1 Cor. 4:20, 21)?

Verse 21 says we have done the opposite of what is directed in Romans 12:21 because we have let evil overcome good. (See Isaiah 5:20, 21.)

Isaiah 1:22 shows that we are mixing bad things and ways of the world with good and valuable things. Samson did the same and lost (Hag. 2:12). Our churches bring the world into their midst, and we play as though our answer to the question posed in Haggai 2:12 is yes instead of no. Repent, America.

Verse 23 says that we have ourselves in the center of our lives and not God's way. We are guilty of loving the world, as described in 1 John 2:15–16.

If we want God to do what he says he will in verse 24, we will have to repent.

Verses 25–31 show that God will straighten us up one way or another. We can choose the easy way or the hard way (1 Cor. 4:21). God will judge us and punish us, as He did Samson, if we don't repent. Which of these two options is the most painful: to confess our sins, repent, and turn back to God or to accept His judgment, punishment, and wrath? Ask Samson. Repent, America. Again, God says, "Repent."

CHAPTER 9

OBEDIENCE = BLESSING, BUT DISOBEDIENCE = CURSE: REPENT OR PERISH

In Deuteronomy 11:1–32, we read about the benefits and importance of obeying God. Note the benefits and promises that God describes in verses 22–25, and note the conditions necessary to receive the blessings or the curses in verses 26–28 (AB).

> 22–25: For if you diligently keep all this commandment which I command you to do, to love the Lord your God, to walk in all His ways, and to cleave to Him—then the Lord will drive out all these nations before you, and you shall dispossess nations greater and mightier than you. Every place upon which the sole of your foot shall tread shall be yours: from the wilderness to Lebanon, and from the River, the river Euphrates, to the western sea [the Mediterranean] your territory shall be. There shall no man be able to stand before you; the Lord your God shall lay the fear and the dread of you upon all the land that you shall tread, as He has said to you.

But verses 26–28 (AB) read as follows:

> Behold, I set before you this day a blessing and a curse—the
> blessing if you obey the commandments of the Lord your
> God which I command you this day; and the curse if you
> will not obey the commandments of the Lord your God,
> but turn aside from the way which I command you this day
> to go after other gods, which you have not known.

In short, if we obey God, we will be blessed. If we disobey God, we will receive a curse. Jesus sums it up in Luke 13:3 and 5—unless we repent, we will perish.

America, we need to repent. To repent means to think differently, to have a change of mind, to do what God says and not what the self says. It is a 180-degree turnaround from the direction we are going.

True repentance will consist of changes in our minds, our hearts, and our wills. God commands us to repent. Acts 17:30 (AB) says, "Such [former] ages of ignorance God, it is true, ignored and allowed to pass unnoticed; but now He charges all people everywhere to repent (to change their minds for the better and heartily to amend their ways, with abhorrence of their past sins).... " Matthew 3:8 says we need to show the fruit of repentance.

In the story of the prodigal son[4] in Luke 15:11–32, note that the younger son came to his father and said, "Give me my portion of goods now." Also remember that Samson told his parents, referring to his first girlfriend, "Get her for me." America has this same "give me" attitude. We want that which pleases us, and we want it now. If you will notice, all kinds of groups of people—the rightists, the leftists, those on welfare, the radicals, the bums, and the rich and the poor—have a "give me" attitude.

The younger son wasted his time and substance in riotous and lustful living as did Samson, and as America has. We have a "give me" philosophy.

The younger son finally got his fill of the lowlife, of living with the swine and of living a life full of recklessness and looseness. Samson lost his strength, and the Spirit of God left him because of his low living and his reckless and loose ways. Just like the younger son and Samson, America is losing her wealth and strength because of all of our reckless and loose living. The son, Samson, and America left God out of their plans and lives.

The nation and many churches have a rebellious attitude toward God.

---

[4] Comments about the prodigal son have been influenced by the writings of Bob Harrington, "the Chaplain of Bourbon Street," and are used by permission.

We do not want to see the truth or hear the truth of God. We even go against God's man if he preaches truth to us. We have a self-will or an *I* problem.

When it comes to repentance, most of the time we do it our way and not God's way. We cry big, hypocritical tears; we are sorry (that we got caught, not that we sinned); and we try to get something for nothing or as cheaply as we can. We try to get in a good or right standing with our relatives, friends, churches, people at work, and everybody everywhere, except with God.

We think that stopping a bad action is repentance. If the drunkard stops drinking and that is all he does, he will go to hell sober. We change only if the change is comfortable. We do not want to totally deny ourselves of our reckless and loose living, and we do not want to follow Jesus.

When we just stop doing a sin and don't really confess it or truly repent of it, we hide our reckless and loose living just in case things go bad or the situation is too uncomfortable for us. For example, a drunkard uses alcohol to hide his problems. He says that he repents, but he still hides a bottle of booze in his cabinet just in case things get too bad for him. He has not really repented of his sins and turned fully to trust in and rely on God. This nation and Christians do a lot of reckless and loose living and very little repenting.

We teach that it is all right to live a little recklessly and loosely now and then if it will make a fellow worker or friend happy. We don't want to offend someone or make him or her uneasy if we tell the truth—and that means that we do not follow Jesus wholeheartedly.

We deceive ourselves when we hide our reckless and loose living and think that nobody knows. Remember, God's spirit is in us, our consciences tell us it's wrong, and Jesus knows our lifestyles. If parents, preachers, bosses, leaders, and so on live reckless and loose lives, then the kids, students, workers, and others all know it. What kind of kids, students, workers, and other people are we going to have if all their leaders live in such a way?

America, we need to do what the younger son did—he came to his senses and realized that he had sinned. And like Samson, we need to confess our sins, repent of them, and cry out to God for forgiveness.

America, 2 Peter 3:9 (AB) says, "The Lord does not delay and is not tardy or slow about what He promises, according to some people's conception of slowness, but He is long-suffering (extraordinarily patient) toward you, not desiring that any should perish, but that all should turn to repentance." God does not want us to perish. Ezekiel 33:11 (AB) says, "Say to them, As I live, says the Lord God, I have no pleasure in the death of the wicked, but rather that the wicked turn from his way and live. Turn back, turn back from your evil ways, for why will you die, O house of Israel?" God does not want to destroy us; He wants us to repent. Remember the command to repent in Acts 17:30.

In 2 Corinthians 4:4 (AB), the Bible says, "For the god of this world has blinded the unbelievers' minds [that they should not discern the truth], preventing them from seeing the illuminating light of the Gospel of the glory of Christ (the Messiah), who is the image and likeness of God." Note that in this verse, *god* (lower case *g*) refers to Satan and not to *God* (uppercase G). We have let things of the world and of the self (our reckless and loose living) blind us to God's plan for us. Our big sins are having too much "self" in our lives and having no trust or faith in God.

In 1 John 1:9, God says that if we confess our sins and our reckless and loose living, God is faithful and just to forgive us. In 1 John 1:8, it says that if we say we have no sin, we deceive ourselves and God's truth is not in us. Remember that Proverbs 28:13 says that if we cover our sins and our reckless and loose living, we will not prosper. But if we confess and forsake our sins and reckless and loose living, God will show us mercy. God wants us to have a broken and contrite heart for Him (Ps. 51:17) and a spirit of humility, not pride (Prov. 16:18).

As a nation, we are like what Jeremiah says about Judah in Jeremiah 2:13 (AB), which says, "For My people have committed two evils: they have forsaken Me, the Fountain of living waters, and they have hewn for themselves cisterns, broken cisterns which cannot hold water." Also, Jeremiah 2:19 (AB) declares, "Your own wickedness shall chasten and correct you, and your backslidings and desertion of faith shall reprove you. Know therefore and recognize that this is an evil and bitter thing: [first,] you have forsaken the Lord your God; [second,] you are indifferent to Me and the fear of Me is not in you, says the Lord of hosts."

Furthermore, Jeremiah 29:10–14 (AB) reads as follows:

> For thus says the Lord, When seventy years are completed for Babylon, I will visit you and keep My good promise to you, causing you to return to this place. For I know the thoughts and plans that I have for you, says the Lord, thoughts and plans for welfare and peace and not for evil, to give you hope in your final outcome. Then you will call upon Me, and you will come and pray to Me, and I will hear and heed you. Then you will seek Me, inquire for, and require Me [as a vital necessity] and find Me when you search for Me with all your

heart. I will be found by you, says the Lord, and I will release you from captivity and gather you from all the nations and all the places to which I have driven you, says the Lord, and I will bring you back to the place from which I caused you to be carried away captive.

We have hope if we will wholeheartedly turn to God. Jeremiah 18:6–10 (AB) says, O house of Israel, can I not do with you as this potter does? says the Lord. Behold, as the clay is in the potter's hand, so are you in My hand, O house of Israel. At one time I will suddenly speak concerning a nation or kingdom, that I will pluck up and break down and destroy it; and if [the people of] that nation concerning which I have spoken turn from their evil, I will relent and reverse My decision concerning the evil that I thought to do to them. At another time I will suddenly speak concerning a nation or kingdom, that I will build up and plant it; and if they do evil in My sight, obeying not My voice, then I will regret and reverse My decision concerning the good with which I said I would benefit them.

Did you notice the "hope," the "promise" God will give us if we repent? Jeremiah 33:3 (AB) reads, "Call to Me and I will answer you and show you great and mighty things, fenced in and hidden, which you do not know (do not distinguish and recognize, have knowledge of and understand)." Do we want God to show us great and mighty things? Repent, America! In the midst of all of this fast-changing information, God can show us things that we do not know.

Isaiah 43:18–19 (AB) declares,

Do not [earnestly] remember the former things; neither consider the things of old. Behold, I am doing a new thing! Now it springs forth; do you not perceive and know it and will you not give heed to it? I will even make a way in the wilderness and rivers in the desert.

If we say yes to God's spirit, which is in us, God will show us new things.

Remember when Samson killed the thousand Philistines with the jawbone of a donkey? At that time, the Philistines had a monopoly on iron. They had all the good weapons, but God did a *new* thing in Samson's situation and showed him a *new* thing with the jawbone. Let us put our trust and hope in God, not the Enemy.

In America, we do not have an oil problem, an economic problem, or a food-shortage problem. We have a *heart* problem, a *priority* problem, and a *spiritual* problem. How can we say we are having financial problems when thousands of people spend millions of dollars on sports? We waste a lot of food, go to all-you-can-eat buffets, and buy all the junk food we can eat. Is there really a food shortage? In addition, we waste gas and oil in the interest of our own comfort.

Again, we have a *priority* problem, a *heart* problem, and a *spiritual* problem; ultimately, we have an *I* problem.

Repent, America, while there is still time. We do not want to get to the point of having a shortage of time. Remember, change is good, but not all change is good. If we change our ways of using oil, food, and money but do not change our hearts for God, the end result will be vanity.

In 2 Chronicles 7:14 (AB), we read, "If My people, who are called by My name, shall humble themselves, pray, seek, crave, and require of necessity My face and turn from their wicked ways, then will I hear from heaven, forgive their sin, and heal their land."

Notice what we as Christians and a nation have to do for God to heal our land. We have to humble ourselves, pray and seek God's face and turn from our wicked ways. If we are willing to do our part, God Guarantees us blessings and healing in our land.

Joshua 24:15–16 (AB) says,

> And if it seems evil to you to serve the Lord, choose for yourselves this day whom you will serve, whether the gods which your fathers served on the other side of the River, or the gods of the Amorites, in whose land you dwell; but as for me and my house, we will serve the Lord. The people answered, Far be it from us to forsake the Lord to serve other gods.

Will we be like Joshua and his house and serve the Lord? Will we not forsake the Lord?

Joshua 24:20 (AB) declares, "If you forsake the Lord and serve strange gods, then He will turn and do you harm and consume you, after having done you good." This verse shows that if we change and start doing good but still forsake God and do not turn our hearts to God, we will still be consumed.

Joshua 24:24 (AB) says, "The people said to Joshua, 'The Lord our God we will serve; His voice we will obey.'" Are we going to do it, America? Are we going to serve and obey God? Are we willing to repent?

In the Amplified Bible, 1 Kings 18:21 reads, "Elijah came near to all the people and said, 'How long will you halt and limp between two opinions? If the Lord is God, follow Him! But if Baal, then follow him.' And the people did not answer him a word." The prophet Elijah asks us, Are you going to serve God or the self?

Proverbs 3:5–6 (AB) says, "Lean on, trust in, and be confident in the Lord with all your heart and mind and do not rely on your own insight or understanding. In all your ways know, recognize, and acknowledge Him, and He will direct and make straight and plain your paths." And Proverbs 16:25 (AB) says, "There is a way that seems right to a man and appears straight before him, but at the end of it is the way of death." Are we going to fully trust God and quit trusting ourselves? Proverbs 16:25 tells us that if we do keep relying on ourselves, the end result will be death. Just ask Samson.

Matthew 26:20–22 and 25 (KJV) says,

> Now when the evening has come, he sat down with the twelve. And as they did eat, he said, "Verily I say unto you, that one of you shall betray me." And they were exceeding sorrowful, and began every one of them to say unto him, "Lord, is it I?" … Then Judas, which betrayed him, answered and said, "Master, is it I?" He said unto him, "Thou hast said."

Did you notice that when Jesus told His disciples that one of them would betray Him, eleven of them said "Lord, is it I?" But Judas called Him "Master," not "Lord."

Luke 23:39–43 (AB) says,

> One of the criminals who was suspended kept up a railing at Him, saying, "Are You not the Christ (the Messiah)? Rescue Yourself and us [from death]!" But the other one reproved

him, saying, "Do you not even fear God, seeing you yourself are under the same sentence of condemnation and suffering the same penalty? And we indeed suffer it justly, receiving the due reward of our actions; but this Man has done nothing out of the way [nothing strange or eccentric or perverse or unreasonable]." Then he said to Jesus, "Lord, remember me when You come in Your kingly glory!" And He answered him, "Truly I tell you, today you shall be with Me in Paradise."

The first thief on the cross tried to use human reasoning with Jesus and got nowhere but death, while the second thief humbled himself, admitted his sin, and addressed Jesus as "Lord." He received salvation and victory.

Are we as a nation going to receive death or victory? The choice is ours. Repent, America.

Mark 10:17–22 (KJV) says,

And when he was gone forth into the way, there came one running, and kneeled to him, and asked him, "Good Master, what shall I do that I may inherit eternal life?" And Jesus said unto him, "Why callest thou me good? There is none good but one, that is, God. Thou knowest the commandments, Do not commit adultery, Do not kill, Do not steal, Do not bear false witness, Defraud not, Honour thy father and mother." And he answered and said unto him, "Master, all these have I observed from my youth." Then Jesus beholding him loved him, and said unto him, "One thing thou lackest: go thy way, sell whatsoever thou hast, and give to the poor, and thou shalt have treasure in heaven: and come, take up the cross, and follow me." And he was sad at that saying, and went away grieved: for he had great possessions.

The rich, young ruler wanted eternal life. "What must I do to receive it?" he asked. Notice that he addressed Jesus as "Good Master," not as "Lord." He was still doing things his way and not committing himself to Jesus. He had the "give me" philosophy. He was also a very good man, even from his youth, but he was not willing to give up himself and follow Jesus wholeheartedly.

From these three passages, we learn that we should not refer to Jesus as a good man, as a master, or as a good master. Some people today call Him "the man upstairs."

To get in with God and His terms and plan, we have to deny ourselves and make Jesus the Lord of our lives. If we obey, we will be blessed and victorious. If we disobey, we will obtain defeat. Repent, America. Repent.

Remember that when we do change for Christ, we will encounter insults and difficulties. We need to continue striving for our goal, to fight, and to not let the hard times get us down or defeat us.

Let's go back to football for a minute. Have you ever noticed how much physical abuse the players go through? But they keep right on playing and going for the gold. We need to be as committed and dedicated to serving Jesus as sports players are to their games.

James 1:12 (AB) says, "Blessed (happy, to be envied) is the man who is patient under trial and stands up under temptation, for when he has stood the test and been approved, he will receive [the victor's] crown of life which God has promised to those who love Him." In 1 Peter 1:6–7 (AB), we read the following:

> [You should] be exceedingly glad on this account, though now for a little while you may be distressed by trials and suffer temptations, so that [the genuineness] of your faith may be tested, [your faith] which is infinitely more precious than the perishable gold which is tested and purified by fire. [This proving of your faith is intended] to redound to [your] praise and glory and honor when Jesus Christ (the Messiah, the Anointed One) is revealed.

If we get through our trials and hard times, we will build up our faith and spiritual strength and win an award far greater and more glorious than any Super Bowl trophy made with man's hands.

Let's go, America. Let's be encouraged by God's spirit and be as God's Word says in 2 Timothy 4:7–8 (AB).

> I have fought the good (worthy, honorable, and noble) fight, I have finished the race, I have kept (firmly held) the faith. [As to what remains] henceforth there is laid up for me the [victor's] crown of righteousness [for being right with God and doing right], which the Lord, the righteous Judge, will

award to me and recompense me on that [great] day—and not to me only, but also to all those who have loved and yearned for and welcomed His appearing (His return).

Finally, in our world today, computers are everywhere and in almost everything. A computer's basic system operates in what in mathematics is called binary or base 2. It is a number system with only two numbers, a 1 and a 0. The computer thinks in either a 1 or a 0—on or off, good or bad, hot or cold, and so on.

When you get to the very bottom of it, God's system is this: You are for me or against me (Matt. 12:30); you are hot or cold (Rev. 3:16); obey or disobey, bless or curse (Deut. 11:26–28); righteous or unrighteous, saved or lost, heaven or hell, the Spirit of Christ or the Spirit of Satan; you accept me (Christ) or reject me (Christ); you have said yes to Christ, or you have said no to Christ.

What are we going to do, America? Obey and get blessed? Disobey and get cursed? Repent and live, or stay unrepentant and die?

Are we going to be a 1 or a 0? The decision is ours to make.

Also in our world today is God's spirit—everywhere and in almost everybody. There are some people who are as Samson was in that God's spirit has left them.

Say yes to God, America.

Repent and live, America.

Isaiah 30:15 (AB) says, "For thus said the Lord God, the Holy One of Israel: In returning [to Me] and resting [in Me] you shall be saved; in quietness and in [trusting] confidence shall be your strength. But you would not...."

Let's say yes to God, America, for salvation and strength. Acts 17:30–31 (AB) says, Such [former] ages of ignorance God, it is true, ignored and allowed to pass unnoticed; but now He charges all people everywhere to repent (to change their minds for the better and heartily to amend their ways, with abhorrence of their past sins), because He has fixed a day when He will judge the world righteously (justly) by a Man whom He has destined and appointed for that task, and He has made this credible and given conviction and assurance and evidence to everyone by raising Him from the dead.

God will forgive our past sins if we will repent. If we do not repent, we will receive the judgment of God as Samson did. Our salvation and our strength is in Jesus Christ, whom God raised from the dead. Let's repent, turn to Jesus, and become victorious, America.

Galatians 6:7–9 (AB) says,

> Do not be deceived and deluded and misled; God will not allow Himself to be sneered at (scorned, disdained, or mocked by mere pretensions or professions, or by His precepts being set aside.) [He inevitably deludes himself who attempts to delude God.] For whatever a man sows, that and that only is what he will reap. For he who sows to his own flesh (lower nature, sensuality) will from the flesh reap decay and ruin and destruction, but he who sows to the Spirit will from the Spirit reap eternal life. And let us not lose heart and grow weary and faint in acting nobly and doing right, for in due time and at the appointed season we shall reap, if we do not loosen and relax our courage and faint.

CHAPTER 10

HOW LONG IS A FOOTBALL GAME?

How long is a football game? I do not know.

A football game is made up of four quarters, each fifteen minutes long. That would make the game sixty minutes, or one hour, long. How many of you have watched a football game that was over in one hour? I never have.

Have you ever watched a bowl game when the teams' scores were tied or just a few points apart with two minutes left? How long did those two minutes last—ten, fifteen, twenty minutes? Have you ever noticed how quickly a game ends when it goes into sudden death overtime and one team scores? A football game does last sixty minutes, as far as the actual playing time, but there are a lot of delays, time-outs, and halftime entertainment, making the game go way past the one hour mark before it is actually over.

Now, how long will it be before Jesus Christ comes back to this earth to take the saints home and rule or reign on this earth for one thousand years? I do not know this either.

In 2 Peter 3:8, the Bible says that one day with the Lord is as a thousand years and that a thousand years are as one day. The old teaching about when the world is coming to an end is as follows:

- From the time of Adam until the flood was approximately two thousand years, or two days, based on 2 Peter 3:8.
- From the time of the flood until the birth of Christ was approximately another two thousand years or two days, making a total of four thousand years or four days from the time of Adam.
- From the time of Christ until the present time is another two thousand years or two days.
- We now have approximately six thousand years or six days from the time of Adam. If you remember, God finished all His creations in six days and rested on the seventh day.

It appears that the sixth day is winding down and that we are waiting for the seventh day or day of rest to come. The seventh day or next one thousand years would be the one-thousand-year reign of Christ on this earth.

One of God's time-outs in the Bible involves King Hezekiah. In 2 Kings 20:1–6, the prophet Isaiah tells Hezekiah that God said that he, Hezekiah, will die. Hezekiah did not like that, and he turned and prayed to God. God heard his prayer and extended his life by fifteen years. You could say that Death received a fifteen-year penalty.

According to God's timetable in 2 Peter 3:8, the seven years of tribulation would take approximately ten minutes. References to the tribulation generally involve adversity, suffering, anguish, or persecution. It is tied to God's process to rid people, a nation, or the world of sin and evil and making them right again.

I have said all this as an example of why we need to be ready and in tune with God at all times because we do not know when our time, either as individuals or as a nation, will be up. Are we living in the final two minutes, or are we in overtime, when we could be defeated in sudden death?

It appears that Samson, with his unconfessed sins, was playing in overtime and lost the game because his enemies scored first; it was sudden death for him. He was still in the game, took a nap, and woke up in defeat.

Proverbs 27:1 (AB) advises us, "Do not boast of [yourself and] tomorrow, for you know not what a day may bring forth." Compare this with Luke 12:19–21 and James 4:13–14. Samson was a free man one day, and the very next day, he was a slave. Is this what we want, America? Then, repent of these unconfessed sins.

In 1 Corinthians 15:51–52, we find that we shall be changed in a moment, in the twinkling of an eye. If we as a nation do not confess our sins and repent, we will receive God's judgment and be handed over to the enemies as Samson was.

Remember, one of the saddest verses in the Bible is found in Judges 16:20, where the Spirit of God, Samson's protection, left Samson, and he did not know that God had left him. He lost his freedom and had to serve the enemies.

Is this what we want, America? Then Repent. Repent; again God says, Repent.

CHAPTER 11

SAMSON, AMERICA, AND THE END TIMES

Could there be any similarity with the life of Samson and the way America is today at the end of time? Remember Romans 15:4 (AB), which says, "For whatever was thus written in former days was *written for our instruction*, that by [our steadfast and patient] endurance and the encouragement [drawn] from the Scriptures we might hold fast to and cherish hope" (emphasis added). And also remember 1 Corinthians 10:11 (AB), which reads, "Now these things befell them by way of a figure [*as an example and warning to us*]; they were written to admonish and fit us for right action by good instruction, we in whose days the ages have reached their climax (their consummation and concluding period)" (emphasis added). God's Word says these events were set as an example and as instructions for us so that we might learn, be encouraged, and have and hold onto our hope. Let us take a look at these and just see what we can see and learn.

First, the following is a little review:

1. Samson's parents wanted a child who they could dedicate to God; the people who helped start America were looking for a land where they could worship and serve God.

2. With Samson beginning his mission in Judges 13:25, the Spirit of the Lord began to move Samson at times; when America was started, the Lord began to move in America at times.

3. Samson had his ups and downs when starting out; and America had her ups and downs starting out.

4. In Judges 15:20, it looks like Samson ruled and reigned for twenty years without any big mistakes like those he made when he first started out; and since 1776, for two hundred years, America has ruled and reigned without some big mistakes. It appears that Samson did well for twenty years, and America did well for two hundred years.

5. How did Samson, after twenty years of "good ruling," fall down to sinning with a harlot or prostitute (Judg. 16:1), becoming guilty of sexual immorality; and how did America, after two hundred years of "good ruling," fall down to sinning by committing sexual immorality and spiritual adultery?

> One answer to the above questions is found in Hosea 4:6–11 (AB): My people are destroyed for lack of knowledge; because you [the priestly nation] have rejected knowledge, I will also reject you that you shall be no priest to Me; seeing you have forgotten the law of your God, I will also forget your children. The more they increased and multiplied [in prosperity and power], the more they sinned against Me; I will change their glory into shame. They feed on the sin of My people and set their heart on their iniquity. And it shall be: Like people, like priest; I will punish them for their ways and repay them for their doings. For they shall eat and not have enough; they shall play the harlot and beget no increase, because they have forsaken the Lord for harlotry; harlotry and wine and new wine take away the heart and the mind and the spiritual understanding.

In verse 6, God says that His people are destroyed for lack of knowledge. Samson as the judge and America as the priestly nation have rejected God's knowledge, wisdom, and Spirit; we have quenched the Holy Spirit (1 Thess. 5:19). We have turned to idol worship; we have *I* in what we do instead of having God in it.

Samson and America are like the church of Ephesus described in Revelation 2:4; we have left our first love—Jesus Christ.

6. Samson had super strength and accomplished many feats with the help of God's Spirit, and with his weakness, he was the best of the lot at that time. Likewise, America is the superpower right now. Over the past two hundred years, we have accomplished many feats with God's help, and as of right now, America is the best of the lot for God's plans.

7. Judges 15:11 (AB) says, "Then 3,000 men of Judah, his own people, went down to the cleft of the rock Etam and said to Samson, 'Have you not known that the Philistines are rulers over us? What is this that you have done to us?' He said to them, 'As they did to me, so have I done to them.'" The three thousand men of Judah were against Samson, upsetting the Philistines (the enemy), and the Israelites seemed content with the Philistines' being rulers over them.

How many churches today get upset if a man of God tries to shake them up, move them out of their comfort zone, and get them on fire for Jesus? The church that is content with being ruled by the Enemy (no serious preaching, no preaching against sins, just food, fun, and fellowship) is like the church of Laodicea described in Revelation 3:14–17 (AB):

> And to the angel (messenger) of the assembly (church) in Laodicea write: These are the words of the Amen, the trusty and faithful and true Witness, the Origin and Beginning and Author of God's creation: I know your [record of] works and what you are doing; you are neither cold nor hot. Would that you were cold or hot! So, because you are lukewarm and neither cold nor hot, I will spew you out of My mouth! For you say, I am rich; I have prospered and grown wealthy, and I am in need of nothing; and you do not realize and understand that you are wretched, pitiable, poor, blind, and naked.

8. In Judges 15:14–16, notice that Samson did a miraculous feat by singlehandedly slaying a thousand men with the jawbone of a donkey. No one from Judah, his own people, came to help him. In

America today, one man of God will preach the truth of God to get a church or people to turn back to God, and most Christians will not get involved and help him.

9. In Judges 15:20 and 16:1, after twenty years of ruling and doing well, Samson was led astray; after two hundred years of America's ruling and doing well, America has been led astray. Both Samson and America let their own false gods lead them astray. Samson's and America's false gods are self and *I*. Matthew 24:24 (AB): "For false Christs and false prophets will arise, and they will show great signs and wonders so as to deceive and lead astray, if possible, even the elect (God's chosen ones)."

10. In Judges 16:4–21, Samson plays with the enemy, bows down to its game plan, and does not take a stand for God. America also gets involved with the enemy; we let them tell us how to play their game, and we do not take a stand for God. Samson and America have deserted their first love. Revelation 2:3–4 (AB) states, "I know you are enduring patiently and are bearing up for My name's sake, and you have not fainted or become exhausted or grown weary. But I have this [one charge to make] against you: that you have left (abandoned) the love that you had at first [you have deserted Me, your first love]."

We have become lukewarm for God. Revelation 3:15–16 (AB) says, "I know your [record of] works and what you are doing; you are neither cold nor hot. Would that you were cold or hot! So, because you are lukewarm and neither cold nor hot, I will spew you out of My mouth!"

Some things to think about and consider are the following: Samson sinned; the enemy captured him; Samson confessed his sins and repented; and God answered his prayer, gave him one more victory, and took him home. Is America going to lose God's Spirit and protection, get captured by the Enemy, confess and repent, and then see the return of Christ? Is Christ going to return and take His saints home before the Enemy captures us? Do we want to confess our sins and repent before or after the Enemy takes us?

11. One of the last stages that a nation or person goes through before God's judgment and wrath come includes engaging in a lifestyle of any and all kinds of sexual immorality.

In the eighteenth and nineteenth chapters of Genesis, God was ready to destroy Sodom and Gomorrah for their sexual wickedness. God took a time-out and showed some mercy to see if Abraham could find ten righteous men. Abraham couldn't, the people did not repent, God's wrath and judgment came, and the cities were destroyed.

The last part of Samson's life was spent with a harlot at Gaza and with Delilah. In Judges 16:4, the word *loved* means to have a sexual desire or expression for someone. Samson was enjoying his sexual appetite when God's judgment came upon him.

How much sexual immorality does America have? While God is showing us His mercy and giving us a time-out, we as a nation need to urgently repent before God's wrath and judgment come to us. Repent, America, while we still have time.

CHAPTER 12

A LITTLE MORE COMPARISON

Here is a little more about number five in the previous chapter about how Samson and America fell from the good style of living to the bad or wrong style of living.

As mentioned in the first chapter of this book, Samson and America are like the unbelievers who know that God is real by His Spirit but have still said no to Him and His ways. We know what God's knowledge, wisdom, and will are, but we, like Samson, have rejected God and said no to Him and His ways.

Hosea 4:7 (AB) declares, "The more they increased *and* multiplied [in prosperity and power], the more they sinned against Me; I will change their glory into shame." We see that as Samson increased in power and sin (rejecting God), God turned Samson's glory into shame. The same thing is happening to America.

Proverbs 6:32 (AB) declares, "But whoever commits adultery with a woman lacks heart and understanding (moral principle and prudence); he who does it is destroying his own life." In other words, a man who commits sexual immorality destroys his own life. Compare that to Hosea 4:1 (AB), which says, "*Hear* the word of the Lord, you children of Israel, for the Lord has a controversy (a pleading contention) with the inhabitants of the land, because there is no faithfulness, love, pity and mercy, or knowledge of God [from personal experience with Him] in the land" (emphasis added). Samson played with the harlots and did not increase in his strength or number—he was still just himself—but his enemies were large in number. Samson and America are much like the people described in Proverbs 30:12 (KJV), which reads, "There is a generation that are pure in their own eyes, and yet is not washed from their filthiness."

Hosea 4:11 (AB) declares, "Harlotry and wine and new wine take away the heart and the mind and the spiritual understanding." This is another reason that Samson backslid and that America is backsliding. With our sinning and spiritual immorality, we are losing our spiritual understanding. America likes its self-gratification of its fleshly appetites, and this dulls our sensitivity to God's Spirit.

We should also note that *unconfessed* sin, even though it brings us success and pleasure for a season (Heb. 11:25), does not bring about a reality or presence of God's approval or blessings. Rather, unconfessed sin brings about the reality and presence of spiritual defeat and God's judgment. Also, the tragedies of sin, unconfessed sin, and unrepented sin separate us from God, and God hides his face from us (Is. 59:1–3).

Remember Psalm 66:18 (AB)—"If I regard iniquity in my heart, the Lord will not hear me"; Proverbs 28:13 (AB)—"He who covers his transgressions will not prosper, but whoever confesses and forsakes his sins will obtain mercy"; and Isaiah 1:15 (AB)—"And when you spread forth your hands [in prayer, imploring help], I will hide My eyes from you; even though you make many prayers, I will not hear. Your hands are full of blood!" Unconfessed sin breaks our relationship with God, as it did with Samson. Also notice what God says in Psalm 32:2–5 (AB):

> Blessed (happy, fortunate, to be envied) is the man to whom the Lord imputes no iniquity and in whose spirit there is no deceit. When I kept silence [before I confessed], my bones wasted away through my groaning all the day long. For day and night Your hand [of displeasure] was heavy upon me; my moisture was turned into the drought of summer. Selah [pause, and calmly think of that]! I acknowledged my sin to You, and my iniquity I did not hide. I said, "I will confess my transgressions to the Lord [continually unfolding the past till all is told]—then You [instantly] forgave me the guilt and iniquity of my sin." Selah [pause, and calmly think of that]!

Proverbs 14:34 (AB) declares, "Uprightness and right standing with God (moral and spiritual rectitude in every area and relation) elevate a nation, but sin is a reproach to any people." We are exalting our "unrighteousness," thereby bringing about disgrace and dishonor to us as a nation. Samson brought dishonor and disgrace to God with his unrighteousness in letting the enemy capture him and giving praise to their god.

Now, back to more of the end-times comparisons. In Judges 14:15, the enemy was about to lose the little game that Samson played with them, the riddle at the wedding feast, so they went to the extreme to find the answer. They did not want to give Samson, God's man and an Israelite, anything. Today, the Enemy does not want to give anything to America, a nation under God, or to Israel. The Enemy will go to any extreme to keep us from any good or from being the winners in any situation.

Even though the enemy got the answer to Samson's riddle by force, they still did not understand what it really meant, who Samson really was, or how his God operated. They were spiritually dead and blind.

People of the world do not really know or understand America or the Spirit of God when we act in a situation according to God's will. They are also spiritually dead and blind. Remember 1 Corinthians 2:14 (AB), which says,

> But the natural, nonspiritual man does not accept or welcome or admit into his heart the gifts and teachings and revelations of the Spirit of God, for they are folly (meaningless nonsense) to him; and he is incapable of knowing them [of progressively recognizing, understanding, and becoming better acquainted with them] because they are spiritually discerned and estimated and appreciated.

In the days of the great tribulation, Israel and the Christians who are born-again believers in Jesus Christ will be punished severely for going against the Enemy, or the Antichrist. The great tribulation will be a period of three and a half years of the seven years of tribulation. It will be a time of unparalleled physical suffering and an intense time of emotional, physical, and spiritual distress. It will kill almost all of life (Matt. 24:15–22).

For more information, re-read Luke 11:23–26 and see pages 41-44 in Chapter 7 of this book.

One last important comparison is this: Samson could not be conquered from without, so the enemy conquered him from within.

Is this what is happening in America today? The enemy cannot conquer America by physical power and strength, so they are conquering us from within. They are taking God out of almost everything, getting rid of moral values, breaking up family relations, and blinding our spiritual eyes.

The death of the strong man Samson, and maybe America, reminds us of the perils and dangers of strength for any man or any nation unless we humble ourselves, confess and repent of our sins, and are controlled by the leading and guidance of the Holy Spirit, the all-wise and loving God and His son Jesus Christ.

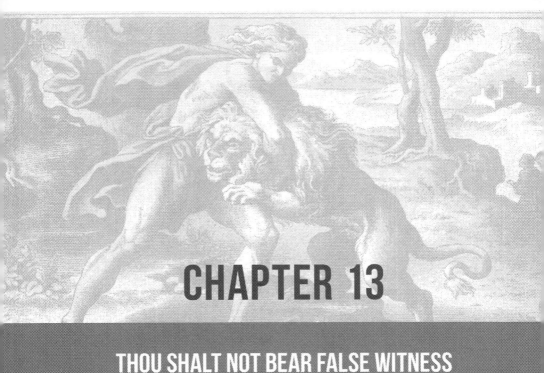

CHAPTER 13

THOU SHALT NOT BEAR FALSE WITNESS

As stated in my biography, my primary natural talent is in numbers and math. I will use some math rules and applications to show some spiritual truths.

I would very strongly recommend that you do not try to use the math application just anywhere in the Bible to prove a point you like without the guidance of the Holy Spirit. I have read topics by people who used parts of the first math application to prove their point, but in the overall spirit of the Bible, they were actually false. I have even tried the math on a few other topics. The result was 2 = 1 or wrong from the Bible teaching, so I quit and did no more.

We will begin with a given valid equation, A = B.

Example: A ($1.00) = B (4 quarters)

Just follow the steps below and see what we came up with for an answer.

$$A = B$$
$$A + A = A + B$$
$$2A = A + B$$

$$
\begin{array}{ccc}
2A-2B & = & A+B-2B \\
2A-2B & = & A-B \\
2\,(A-B) & = & 1\,(A-B) \\
(A-B) & & (A-B) \\
2 & = & 1
\end{array}
$$

Given $\quad$ A = B

Now add A to both sides and you get A + A = A + B

Remember the Golden Rule in math is:

"Do unto one side of the equation as you would unto the other."

Now regroup the A's on the left side and you have 2A = A + B

Now subtract 2B from both sides and you have 2A − 2B = A + B − 2B

Regroup the B's on the right hand side and you get 2A − 2B = 1A − 1B (+ 1B and − 2B = − 1B)

Now factor both sides and get 2 (A−B) = 1 (A−B)
Divide both sides by A − B; the A − B cancels out on the left side leaving 2, and on the right side leaving 1, and we now have 2 = 1

Where did we go wrong? We followed the rules, but we came up with the wrong answer of 2 = 1.

One of the ten commandments in math is *Thou shalt not divide by zero.*

If A = B, what is A−B? If A = $1.00 and B = 4 quarters, then A−B or $1.00 − 4 quarters = zero.

When we divided both sides by (A−B), we were actually dividing by zero, which is a math violation, and we came up with the wrong or false answer of 2 = 1. We went wrong by calling zero (A−B).

To apply this to America and Samson, we find that America, like Samson, will change the thoughts of our hearts that are against God's Word and call our wrongdoing a word or phrase that "tickles our ears" and seemeth right unto man, the result of which is death.

When Samson saw his first girlfriend, she pleased his flesh and he lusted after her, but he called it love.

In America, we have all kinds of sexual lust that we call love or doing what pleases self. We are deceiving ourselves when we believe that 2 = 1 or lust = love.

When Samson retaliated against the Philistines, he thought his way (self) was right. His way (self) was God's way, but again, he believed 2 = 1 and he was wrong again. In America, we believe our way, pleasing self, is the right way. We believe 2 = 1 and we deceive ourselves. God says we are to die to self (see Matt. 16:24–26 AB).

When Samson was playing with sin, lust, and deceitfulness or lying to Delilah, he was having a great time and believing 2 = 1. He was wrong, and he lost.

We in America play with our lust and deceitfulness and believe the lies we tell ourselves. God's Word says to avoid the appearance of sin, but we say it's all right, as long as we don't fully commit the wrong deed. Again, we change our lusts or sins and call them a name that seems right to us. We believe 2 = 1, deceive ourselves, and say it's all right.

One example is the sin of abortion. God's Word says thou shalt not kill or murder. To ease our consciences we change the word *kill* to *abortion* or 2 = 1 and we are wrong again.

Notice what God says in Gen. 2:16–17, "And the Lord God commanded the man, saying, Of every tree of the garden thou mayest freely eat: But of the tree of the knowledge of good and evil, thou shalt not eat of it: for in the day that thou eatest thereof thou shalt surely die." Compare that with what the serpent (Satan) said to Eve in Gen. 3:1, 4–5.

> Now the serpent was more subtle than any beast of the field which the Lord God had made. And he said unto the woman, Yea, hath God said, Ye shall not eat of every tree of the garden? And the serpent said unto the woman, Ye shall not surely die: For God doth know that in the day ye eat thereof, then your eyes shall be opened, and ye shall be as gods, knowing good and evil.

The serpent or Satan quoted God incorrectly, lied to Eve, deceived her, and made it look as though 2 = 1 was the right way to go. When you read the rest of the story in Gen. 3:7–24, you will see that Adam, Eve, and the serpent or Satan received God's curse and penalty for disobeying God, believing false ideas, believing 2 = 1, and trusting in self instead of God for their success.

In addition, if you noticed, no one admitted to being wrong, no one confessed his sins much less repented of his sins.

Today, we are still reaping some of the consequences of the sins committed by Adam and Eve, and when we want to do what is wrong, we tell ourselves a lie when we say no one will get hurt but me. Once again, we believe the false and wrong answer of 2 = 1.

In Isaiah 5:8–25, you find five woes visited upon the unfaithful Israelites, and in verse 20, which reads, "Woe unto them that call evil good, and good evil; that put darkness for light, and light for darkness; that put bitter for sweet, and sweet for bitter!" they believed in 2 = 1. They called good evil, and they called evil good. They relied on self, a way that seemeth right unto men, instead of God.

We in America need to search our lives and spirits, find out what lies we have believed and relied upon that are not in line with the truth of God. We need to repent of them and turn back to God's ways if we want to survive as a people and as a nation.

Also notice in 1 Corinthians 6:18, in just a few words God gives us a command to flee sexual immorality. Man does not like God's commands, so we write several pages about when and why it is all right to believe a lie and false teaching that 2 = 1.

There is a principle in math that reads *Numbers never lie, it's the man who uses them.* Likewise, God's Word, the Holy Bible, never lies. It is man who uses the Bible and twists God's Word to obtain the wrong results.

Mankind has difficulty giving up our wrong ways for God's way—the Truth. Here are a few things to think about pertaining to the Truth.

The truth hurts, but those lies kill.

The truth hurts only if it is supposed to hurt.

The truth will set you free, but first it might make you miserable.

Remember that white is a symbol of something that is pure; therefore, a white lie is a pure lie.

As individuals, as Christians, as a nation, we need to turn to Jesus Christ, who is THE TRUTH so we will be able to recognize and overcome the lies and false teachings of the world.

CHAPTER 14

A MORE EXCELLENT, BETTER BY FAR, AND HIGHEST WAY!

Some time ago I took a class in natureophy, a class designed to treat physical illness with natural remedies instead of with medicine, under the teachings of Dr. Joel Robbins. As we were going through the class, a lot of things Dr. Robbins said or taught us about the physical body—what made it run well or what made it run not as well—would make me think more of the spiritual application—what would make me spiritually stronger or what I do to weaken myself spiritually—than the physical aspect of it.

Some of the things I thought were as follows: If a person has a habit of consuming sweets, pop, coffee, pastries, etc., and either defends his situation to consume them or just can't, or better yet "won't" give them up, does that tie in with some sin he accepts that he does or does not do, that he "won't" give up or a good deed he refuses to do? Also, if he refuses to die to self by consuming the junk foods regularly, would that mean he is not totally sold out to God?

If we won't eat the proper physical foods, will we not take the proper spiritual food or action needed to comply with God's will, as opposed to man's will?

We know that sugar and caffeine deplete the body of B and C vitamins.

We tell ourselves, if we take extra B and C vitamins, we can go have a soda pop and candy bar. We think everything will balance out and be all right.

But, the Bible says that evil or bad corrupts the good. In I Corinthians 15:33 and in Ezekiel 33:12-16, it says the day in which we sin or do wrong, our righteousness is no good and will not cancel out the bad.

So, do we deceive ourselves by thinking if we sin or do wrong that an extra hour of Bible reading will cancel it out? Yes.

What we are really doing by taking more vitamins with the junk food or more Bible reading with our shortcomings is avoiding the responsibility of our actions and avoiding the truth.

One week before the final semester, Dr. Robbins told us to bring our Bibles when we came to class the following week. He was going to teach on the importance of how your attitude affects your overall physical condition. A few examples can be found in Prov. 12:25, Prov. 14:30, Prov. 15:13, and Prov. 17:22. As the Bible says in Prov. 17:22a, "A merry heart doeth good like a medicine." The main ingredient we need in our lives and souls is the love of God.

In the twelfth chapter of 1 Corinthians, Paul talks about spiritual gifts and how to grow and be useful in the Body of Christ. He ends the chapter by saying he will show us a more excellent way. It begins in chapter thirteen and is the way of love.

There are four words in Greek for the word *love*. First is *phileo*, which is brotherly love; the second is *eros*, which is sensual and selfish love; the third is *storge*, which is family love; and the fourth, which is what Paul was talking, about is *agape* love, which is a self-sacrificing unconditional love and the highest characteristic of God: I love you even if you do not love me.

As you read Chapter 13 of 1 Corinthians from the Amplified Bible, notice the contrast and significance of love in verses 1–3. In verses 4–7, notice the characteristics and perfect way of love. Notice in verses 8–13, the consistency, and the degree of firmness and indestructibility of love.

> If I [can] speak in the tongues of men and [even] of angels, but have not love [that reasoning, intentional, spiritual devotion such as is inspired by God's love for and in us], I am only a noisy gong or a clanging cymbal. And if I have prophetic powers—that is, the gift of interpreting the divine will and purpose; and understand all the secret truths and mysteries and possess all knowledge, and if I have (sufficient) faith so

that I can remove mountains but have not love [God's love in me] I am nothing—a useless nobody. Even if I dole out all that I have [to the poor in providing] food and if I surrender my body to be burned [or in order that I may glory], but have not love [God's love in me], I gain nothing.

Love endures long and is patient and kind; love never is envious nor boils over with jealousy; is not boastful or vainglorious, does not display itself haughtily. It is not conceited—arrogant and inflated with pride; it is not rude (unmannerly) and does not act unbecomingly. Love [God's love in us] does not insist on its own right, or its own way for it is not self-seeking; it is not touchy or fretful or resentful; it takes no account of the evil done to it—pays no attention to a suffered wrong. It does not rejoice at injustice and unrighteousness, but rejoices when right and truth prevail. Love bears up under anything and everything that comes, is ever ready to believe the best of every person, its hopes are fadeless under all circumstances and it endures everything [without weakening].

Love never fails—never fades out or becomes obsolete or comes to an end. As for prophecy [that is, the gift of interpreting the divine will and purpose] it will be fulfilled and pass away; as for tongues they will be destroyed and cease; as for knowledge, it will pass away [that is it will lose its value and be superseded by truth]. For our knowledge is fragmentary (incomplete and imperfect), and our prophecy (our teaching) is fragmentary (incomplete and imperfect). But when the complete and perfect [total] comes, the incomplete and imperfect will vanish away—become antiquated, void, and superseded. When I was a child I talked like a child, I thought like a child, I reasoned like a child; now that I have become a man, I am done with childish ways and have put them aside. For now we are looking in a mirror that gives only a dim (blurred) reflection [of reality as in a riddle or enigma], but then [when perfection comes] we shall see in reality and face to face! Now I know in part (imperfectly);

but then I shall know and understand fully and clearly even in the same manner as I have been fully and clearly known and understood [by God].

And so Faith, Hope, Love abide ["Faith," conviction and belief respecting man's relation to God and divine things; "Hope," joyful and confident expectation of eternal salvation; "Love," true affection for God and man, growing out of God's love for and in us], these three, but the greatest of these is Love.

In math, there is a rule that states two negatives make a positive. Also in math, pertaining to the number scale, the term *negative* means to go to the left or be lesser in value. Positive means go to the right or increase in value.

I must again emphasize not to try these math principles just anyplace in the Bible unless you are guided by the Holy Spirit. Otherwise, you will come up with the wrong or false results of 2= 1.

We are going to put two negatives in the verses and have it come out positive. The first negative is to change the word "love," meaning God's love, to "lust," meaning man's love. The second negative is to reverse the verb. If the verb is "is," it becomes "is not," if it is "is not," it becomes "is," etc. Now the way to read I Corinthians 13 with two negatives is as follows:

Though I speak with the tongues of men and of angels, but have lust, I have become a sounding brass or a clanging cymbal. And though I have the gift of prophecy, and understand all mysteries and all knowledge, and though I have all faith, so that I could remove mountains, but have lust, I am nothing. And though I bestow all my goods to feed the poor, and though I give my body to be burned, but have lust, it profits me nothing.

Lust does not suffer long and is not kind; lust does envy; lust does parade itself; is puffed up, does behave rudely, does seek its own; is provoked, thinks evil, does rejoice in iniquity, but rejoices not in the truth, bears not all things, believes not all things, hopes not all things, endures not all things.

> Lust always fails. But whether there are prophecies, they will fail; whether there are tongues, they will cease, whether there is knowledge, it will vanish away. For we know in part and we prophesy in part. But when that which is perfect has come, then that which is in part will be done away.
>
> When I was a child, I spoke as a child, I understood as a child, I thought as a child; but when I became a man, I put away childish things. For now we see in a mirror dimly, but then face to face. Now I know in part, but then I shall know just as I also am known.

And now abstain from doubts, fears, lust, these three; but the worst of these is lust.

As you read about man's love (or what is more rightly called *lust*), notice the nothingness of lust in verses 1–3; and notice the characteristics of lust, the error of lust, and the imperfect way of lust in verses 4–7. In verses 8–13, notice the fickleness, the instability, and the destruction of lust.

Once again, in math, there is a law that states if A = B and B = C, then A = C. For example, (A) four quarters = (B) ten dimes, (B) ten dimes = (C) one dollar. Therefore, (A) four quarters = (C) one dollar.

One more time—do not use the math formula to prove what you want unless led by the Holy Spirit. There is a group out in the religious world that teaches a false belief from the Bible, and they use the above system to prove their false belief.

In math, if A = B and B = C, then A = C. A = Jesus, B = God, C = love.

In John 10:30, Jesus said He is God; In 1 John 4:8, it says God is love. So, if Jesus is God, and God is love, then Jesus is love.

Now read the thirteenth chapter of 1 Corinthians (KJV) and substitute the name "Jesus" for the word "love." It reads as follows:

> Though I speak with the tongues of men and of angels, but have not Jesus, I have become a sounding brass or a clanging cymbal. And though I have the gift of prophecy, and understand all mysteries and all knowledge, and though I have all faith, so that I could remove mountains, but have not Jesus, I am nothing. And though I bestow all my goods

to feed the poor, and though I give my body to be burned, but have not Jesus, it profits me nothing.

Jesus suffers long and is kind; Jesus does not envy; Jesus does not parade Himself; Jesus is not puffed up. Jesus does not behave rudely; does not seek His own; is not provoked, thinks no evil; Jesus does not rejoice in iniquity, but rejoices in the truth; Jesus bears all things, believes all things, hopes all things, endures all things.

Jesus never fails. But whether there are prophecies, they will fail; whether there are tongues, they will cease, whether there is knowledge, it will vanish away. For we know in part and we prophesy in part. But when that which is perfect has come, then that which is in part will be done away.

When I was a child, I spoke as a child, I understood as a child, I thought as a child; but when I became a man, I put away childish things. For now we see in a mirror dimly, but then face to face. Now I know in part, but then I shall know just as I also am known.

And now abide in faith, hope, Jesus, these three; but the greatest of these is Jesus.

Again, as you read this, notice the importance and significance of the Man in the Glory, Jesus, in verses 1–3. In reading verses 4–7, notice the characteristics and perfect way of Jesus. Just stop and ask yourself, how many of these fifteen characteristics of Jesus do you have in your life. In verses 8–13, notice the consistency, firmness, and indestructibility of Jesus, the Savior of the world.

Now, compare Samson's life and lifestyle with the second 15 points of love, lust. Notice in verse two, Samson had the strength to remove city gates and slay one thousand men, but he really did not gain anything for God because of his lust and selfish ways. On his deathbed, he repented and cried out to God, and God gave him the strength to tear down the Philistines' house and he did accomplish something for God.

Also notice some of the characteristics of lust that Samson had. He didn't suffer long, he was envious, he was puffed up, and he did not endure all things. In verse 8, notice that it says lust always fails. Samson had lust and he failed.

I made up a paraphrase about verse 11: When I was a child, I spoke like a child, I understood as a child, I thought like a child, but when I became a man, I still acted like a child. This describes how Samson was when he grew up and acted on lust his instead of God's love.

Can you see America in Samson? With our lust, our selfishness, our ways that seemeth right unto man, and we are still failing.

In verses 2 and 3, we have a lot of knowledge about a lot of things, we understand a lot of hidden mysteries of science, we give our goods to help poor people and nations, but we don't have God's love in us as a whole, and it profits us nothing.

Verse 4 says lust does not suffer long. Are we like the child that grew up and was still a child (see paraphrase of verse 11 above)?

The way a baby is, is as follows, "I want what I want when I want it, or I will bawl and squall to high heavens until I get what I want."[5]

As a nation as a whole, we need to give up our baby attitude; our childish, selfish ways; and grow up and mature by repenting of our selfish ways and accepting God's love and Jesus Christ's way of love.

In verse 13, where it mentions faith, hope, and love, notice the following. Abide in—

Faith—we are saved by faith; without faith it is impossible to please God; faith is the victory that overcomes the world; but *love*—Jesus is the greatest.

Hope—we are saved by hope; our hope gives us strength to overcome problems in life; but *love*—Jesus is the greatest. Also, remember that all of our faith and belief, our hopes, our good deeds, are no good, of no eternal value if we do not have Jesus.

When this old world is gone, and all the saints are in heaven, there will be no need for hope or faith, but there will be a lot of loving and Jesus. Notice what God says in Jeremiah 31:3 (KJV), "The Lord hath appeared of old unto me, saying, Yea, I have loved thee with an everlasting love: therefore with loving kindness have I drawn thee."

To get rid of our selfish ways, out doubts, and our fears, look at 1 John 4:18–19 (AB), which says, "There is no fear in love [dread does not exist], but

---

[5] A quote from the sermon "Slop Bucket Repentance" by Reverend Bob Harrington; used by permission.

full-grown (complete, perfect) love turns fear out of doors *and* expels every trace of terror! For fear brings with it the thought of punishment, and [so] he who is afraid has not reached the full maturity of love [is not yet grown into love's complete perfection]. We love *Him*, because He first loved us."

God's supreme love, self-sacrificing love, and unconditional love is found in the following verse, which is known as the Gospel in a nutshell. "For God so loved the world, that he gave his only begotten Son, that whosoever believeth in him should not perish, but have everlasting life" (John 3:16 KJV).

As a nation, let's turn and receive God's love; we will be happy we did.

CHAPTER 15

A COMPACT SUMMARY AND ANALYSIS

A short summary is this: We, as a nation, need to confess and repent of our sins and get back to clinging to and relying on Jesus Christ instead of man's way or ourselves. Remember, Samson started out well and good and provided a good example for us on the subversive power and influence of sin in his life and the restoration and healing power of God's forgiveness, love, and grace.

Are we, as Americans, ready to confess all of our sins, especially all of our "rely on self" sins, repent of them, and turn to Christ for our healings? Our sins blind us from God's truths and ways and will eventually grind us to our deaths if we don't confess them.

James 4:4 declares, "You [are like] unfaithful wives [having illicit love affairs with the world and breaking your marriage vow to God]! Do you not know that being the world's friend is being God's enemy? So whoever chooses to be a friend of the world takes his stand as an enemy of God." Samson's life shows us what will happen to us when we compromise our beliefs and become friends with the world. Samson kept ignoring God's warnings to repent and come back to Him (God).

In Revelation 2:18–29, John talks about the church in Thyatira. They were growing in faith, but the believers were allowing and tolerating false doctrines. Notice what verses 21–23 (AB) say.

> I gave her time to repent, but she has no desire to repent of her immorality [symbolic of idolatry] *and* refuses to do so. Take note: I will throw her on a bed of anguish], and those who commit adultery with her [her paramours] I will bring down to pressing distress *and* severe affliction, unless they turn away their minds from conduct [such as] hers *and* repent of *their* doings. And I will strike her children (her proper followers) dead [thoroughly exterminating them]. And all the assemblies (churches) shall recognize *and* understand that I am He Who searches minds (the thoughts, feelings, and purposes) and the [inmost] hearts, and I will give to each of you [the reward for what you have done] as your work deserves.

God gave them time to repent, and then the day of judgment set in on them.

Let's repent, America, while God is still giving us time and get back in line with God and God's way instead of man's way. Let's make this choice one of repentance and hope. Experience a nation with revival and God's grace and love. Are we really willing to put forth the effort to survive as a nation? Will we be one nation under God or one nation under?

The choice is yours!

Author's note: Read the Book of Jonah and see how a sinful and evil nation was saved from God's wrath and judgment by repenting.

Let's go for it, America!

CHAPTER 16

FOR THE NONBELIEVERS AND UNSAVED

(those who have said no to God's Spirit)

If your life is full of darkness and you have never said yes to God's Spirit and if you would like for the light to come into your life, accept Jesus Christ as the Lord and Savior of your life, and receive an eternal victory to live forever with Christ, here is all you need to do.

First, acknowledge and admit your sins to God. Romans 3:23 (AB) declares that we have all sinned—"since all have sinned and are falling short of the honor and glory which God bestows and receives." Romans 6:23a (AB) gives the price for our sins—"For the wages which sin pays is death."

Second, you need to repent of your sins. "So repent (change your mind and purpose); turn around and return [to God], that your sins may be erased (blotted out, wiped clean), that times of refreshing (of recovering from the effects of heat, of reviving with fresh air) may come from the presence of the Lord" (Acts 3:19 AB). When you truly repent, you will stop turning your back to God and stop saying no to His Spirit that is within you, and you will seek God's face and say yes to His Spirit that is within you.

Third, believe in, trust in, and rely on Jesus Christ. Acts 16:30–31 (AB) tells you how to be saved. "And he brought them out (of the dungeon) and said, Men, what is it necessary for me to do that I may be saved? And they answered, Believe in the Lord Jesus Christ (give yourself up to Him, take yourself out of your own keeping and entrust yourself into His keeping) and you will be saved, (and this applies both to) you and your household as well."

Remember, God loves you. Romans 5:8 (AB) reads, "But God shows and clearly proves His (own) love for us by the fact that while we were still sinners, Christ (the Messiah, the Anointed One) died for us." John 3:16 (AB) supports this with, "For God so greatly loved and dearly prized the world that He (even) gave up His only begotten (unique) Son, so that whoever believes in (trusts in, clings to, relies on) Him shall not perish (come to destruction, be lost) but have eternal (everlasting) life." Further, 2 Peter 3:9 (AB) declares that He is not willing that anyone should perish but that everyone should repent—"The Lord does not delay and is not tardy or slow about what He promises, according to some people's conception of slowness, but He is long-suffering (extraordinarily patient) toward you, not desiring that any should perish, but that all should turn to repentance."

John 14:6 declares that the only way to God is through His Son, Jesus Christ. Receive eternal life today, replace the darkness in your life with light, and remember that Jesus is the light (John 1:9) by making Jesus Christ the Lord and Savior of your life. This is a choice that only you can make; no one can make it for you.

If you say yes to Jesus, you get what God declares in John 3:36a (AB): "And he who believes in (has faith in, clings to, relies on) the Son has (now possesses) eternal life." If you say no to Jesus, you get what God declares in John 3:36b (AB): "But whoever disobeys (is unbelieving toward, refuses to trust in, disregards, is not subject to) the Son will never see (experience) life, but (instead) the wrath of God abides on him. (God's displeasure remains on him; His indignation hangs over him continually.)"

If you say yes to Jesus (John 3:36a), you will spend eternal life with Him in heaven.

If your answer to Jesus is no (John 3:36b), you will be separated from God and Jesus forever in a place the Bible calls hell.

Remember, you have only one decision to make, and that is, "Will you say yes to Jesus?" If you do not say yes to Jesus, you have already said no to Him. Matthew 12:30 declares, "He who is not with Me [definitely on My side] is against Me, and he who does not [definitely] gather with Me and for My side scatters" (AB).

CHAPTER 17

A WORD TO BORN-AGAIN BELIEVERS

At the beginning of this book, we talked about God's Spirit within us. After we become Christians, we can still say yes or no to God's laws and rules—to His Spirit within us.

Too many Christians and too many churches do things and hold events that seem right to man and the flesh, much as Samson did. We need to repent for our fleshly appetites and put Jesus Christ back at the center of our lives and churches.

God told His people not to marry foreign women because the women would bring their foreign gods and false teachings with them and bring down God's man, God's people. Today, there are too many foreign gods and false teachings in our churches. We have a lot of good things in our lives and churches, but these good things, these activities, these false gods replace our worship with the true God and Jesus Christ.

There is nothing wrong with getting married, buying land, or raising cattle. However, if these good things interfere with our commitment and worship to God, they become wrong and false teachers to us. Read Luke 14:15–24.

How many of us Christians have gone to a church that canceled a worship service on Sunday night so its members could watch the Super

Bowl? We deceive ourselves and believe our own lies when we say there are some people who would never come to church under normal circumstances, so watching football will make them come to church. Or we say, "If one person gets saved, isn't it worth it?"

Ask yourself this question: "When was the last time you canceled the Super Bowl and worshipped God for four hours?"

In reality, we are saying, *Let's bring some worldly, fleshly, false teaching into the church so the world will come and bring its ways into the church.* We get infected with the world's way as Samson did instead of the world's getting infected with God's way. God said for us to go into the world (Matt. 28:19) and not to conform to the ways of the world (Rom. 12:2). If we can win one person to Jesus by using man's way, just think how many more we could bring to Jesus if we did it God's way. Samson rationalized using his way instead of God's way, and in the end, he lost.

This is one example of false teachings or false gods that we bring into the church, and a lot of them we marry. Can you think of other false teachings in our churches?

Let's bring the Holy Spirit back into the church, die to self and man's way, and get back to true worship for God. We bring too much of the world into the church and not enough of God into the world. We operate too much like Samson—our way instead of God's way.

Romans 12:2 says that we Christians are not to be conformed to the ways of the world. In Haggai 2:13, God's Word declares that if we bring the unclean, unholy, worldly, or false teachings into the church along with the clean and holy things, the clean and holy become infected with the unclean or worldly things. Remember, Samson played with sin and unclean things; they replaced the Spirit of God in him, and Samson lost his mission or calling.

Let's give up these Samson or man-made ideas and get repentant hearts, broken spirits, and broken and contrite hearts for God. Let's start a revival for God and our nation, and let it begin in you.

Don't worry about the big sinners in the world. God will take care of them. Pray for them; get back to spreading the way, the truth, the life, and the light—Jesus Christ. Let's show less of our love or lust and display more of the love of Jesus Christ. Pray for a greater love and commitment to Jesus Christ.

Here's one final thought for us to learn from the events of old. Remember Job? He had a bad case of *I*-itis. He had a lot of *I, me, my,* and *mine* in the answers he gave to his friends. Not until God started dealing with him did Job start to be humble.

Job 42:6 says Job finally dies to self and repents. Job's captivity was being under Satan's control, which God allowed. In verse 10, the Lord turned the captivity of Job and blessed him when he prayed for his friends with twice as much as he had lost. Are we willing to confess our sins, die to self, repent, and return to God? Read and do 2 Chronicles 30:9.

Author's note: Remember from the Introduction the funny little joke about Samson bringing down the whole house? If we as a nation do not repent and turn back to God, we will bring down the whole nation of America, and that will not be very funny.

P.S. I read where in the Library of Congress is a plaque which reads "When a nation forgets its beginnings, it begins to decay."

Have we forgot our beginning as a nation or our new beginning in Christ?

Remember if self or sin rules us, it will destroy us.

CHAPTER 18

A WORD TO THE CHURCHES AND PASTORS

We know that when a man or woman commits adultery, he or she is being unfaithful to his or her mate and is guilty of breaking his or her marriage vow, commitment, and covenant and being unfaithful to it. Some of the Old Testament prophets used the term *adultery* and applied it to God's people as in *spiritual adultery*, meaning "to be unfaithful to God" or "serving and worshiping other gods, people, or things, instead of God Himself."

Remember, God warned His people not to marry foreign, strange, or outside people or people who worshiped other gods because they would bring their foreign or strange beliefs with them and would influence God's people in the wrong way. The prophet Jeremiah declared that God's people were guilty of spiritual adultery in chapter 3, verses 6–10, which reads as follows from the Amplified Bible:

> Moreover, the Lord said to me [Jeremiah] in the days of Josiah the king [of Judah], Have you seen what that faithless and backsliding Israel has done—how she went up on every high hill and under every green tree and there played the harlot? And I said, After she has done all these things, she will return to Me; but she did not return, and her faithless

and treacherous sister Judah saw it. And I saw, even though [Judah knew] that for this very cause of committing adultery (idolatry) I [the Lord] had put faithless Israel away and given her a bill of divorce; yet her faithless and treacherous sister Judah was not afraid, but she also went and played the harlot [following after idols]. And through the infamy and unseemly frivolity of Israel's whoredom [because her immorality mattered little to her], she polluted and defiled the land, [by her idolatry] committing adultery with [idols of] stones and trees. But in spite of all this, her faithless and treacherous sister Judah did not return to Me in sincerity and with her whole heart, but only in sheer hypocrisy [has she feigned obedience to King Josiah's reforms], says the Lord.

Also, in the prophet Hosea's book, God tells His people that their being unfaithful to Him is just like a man's committing adultery makes him unfaithful to his wife. In the fourth chapter of Hosea, he tells about the sinful nature and unfaithfulness (spiritual adultery) of His people.

How many foreign, strange, outside-of-God's ways, and instances of unfaithfulness do our churches bring into them? And how often do we start to practice them, worship them, and get our eyes off of the real truth, Jesus Christ?

Notice some parallels between many of today's churches and what Proverbs says about strange or foreign women (women who hold a false belief and/or worship false gods). Proverbs 5 asserts that the lips of a strange woman are sweet like honey to lead a man astray but that her feet go down to death (verses 3–5).

Compare that with the man-made ideas or false teachings that are sweet to our ears but bring us down to spiritual defeat or death. In Proverbs 6:20–24, God says that if we keep His commandments, they will protect from the false teaching. In verses 27–32, we find out that a man cannot commit adultery without getting burned and that he also lacks understanding and destroys his own soul.

Notice that the last part of verse 26 declares that the adulteress will hunt for a man's life. Remember, Delilah kept her commitment to her false god and finally got Samson's life for the enemy. If our churches keep committing spiritual adultery with the false teachings of man, the Enemy will capture us to serve him. We need to be as committed to the true and only God as Delilah was to the false god. Likewise, a church cannot commit spiritual adultery without receiving the penalties for doing it, including that the church loses its spiritual understanding (see Hosea 4:11).

In Chapter 7 of Proverbs, notice all of the deceitful ways that the strange woman or foreigner uses to tickle a man's ear to get him to stumble and fall from his faithfulness. Can you find some of the teaching or ways in the church that are sweet and pleasing to the ways of man—the eyes, the ears, the flesh and get our commitment away from God and to man's way?

With these sweet, deceitful ways that seem right to man, of which the end is death, we become more unfaithful to God. As in Proverbs 29:3b, a man wastes money in the company of harlots, and the church wastes money on the false or foreign teachings and ways of spiritual adultery in which they engage.

Samson liked the sweet deceit of the women in his life, and he also liked his ways, his false ideas, more than he liked God's ways. Samson paid a big price for putting himself in first place in his life instead of God. He lost God's Spirit, his eyesight, and served the enemy instead of God.

In Proverbs 30:18–20, there are four things the writer does not understand or know. One of these is how a woman can commit adultery and then say, "I have done nothing wrong." Likewise, how can a church commit spiritual adultery and then say it is not wrong?

One final word to the unbelievers, Christians, and the church: God still loves us, but He is serious about His ways and no other ways. He wants us to repent and come back to Him. Note what Jeremiah 6:16 (NLT) says,

> This is what the Lord says:
> Stop at the crossroads and look around.
> Ask for the old, godly way, and walk in it.
> Travel its path, and you will find rest for your souls.
> But you reply, 'No, that's not the road we want!'

Also, Jeremiah 5:30–31 (AB) states,

> An appalling and horrible thing [bringing desolation and destruction] has come to pass in the land: The prophets prophesy falsely, and the priests exercise rule at their own

hands *and* by means of the prophets. And My people love to have it so! But what will you do when the end comes?

When we "compromise" the word of God, it causes "corruption" of the word of God, which in turn causes "confusion" of the word of God, causing every man to do what is right in his own eyes. See Proverbs 16:2

Let's give up all of our ways, our false ways, and be faithful and committed to the true way—Jesus Christ, the way, the truth, and the life. Repent and live, America—while we still have time.

A Paraphrase of Matthew 5:29

If thy "I" causes you to sin, cast it out and repent. It is better to die to self, than to have the whole body and soul cast into hell.

AUTHOR BIOGRAPHY

Stephen Ray Williams is a retired electrician. Born again at the age of ten he is gifted with a natural talent and magnificent aptitude for math. Williams was able to show and display his natural gift at an early age, teaching a second semester math class at the age of eleven. His logical and analytical mind also brought him a chess trophy (third in the State in the Junior Division) at the age of thirteen and an award for the world's largest unofficial "Magic Math Square" in his ninth grade science fair at the age of fourteen. As Williams' extensive knowledge was acknowledged, opportunities to share it were in demand. He taught one class in Number Theory at the Oral Roberts University in his mid-twenties with two math formulas he discovered. Williams had a math formula copyrighted. He also earned a Doctor of Naturopathy Certificate, a drug-free medical treatment. He won a baseball trophy in his teens. He played a cornet for five years. He played fiddle for five years. He square danced for seven years, involved in two square dance exhibitions, and a total of fifteen clubs. Williams has written one praise song, one hymn, and one fiddle hoedown. He has written several poems about his best friend (an orange tabby cat named "Tiger Ray"). The poems have been published in eight books, two of which went international; one became a song and got up to a national release. He has also won four trophies for his poems about Tiger Ray!

Williams' favorite place for relaxation and vacation is the Billy Graham Training Center at the Cove in Ashville, North Carolina.

Printed in the United States
By Bookmasters